NEW WAYS TO TELL THE OLD, OLD STORY

NEW WAYS
TO TELL THE OLD,
OLD STORY

Choosing & Using Bible Stories with Children & Youth

Delia Halverson

Abingdon Press

Nashville

NEW WAYS TO TELL THE OLD, OLD STORY: CHOOSING AND USING
BIBLE STORIES WITH CHILDREN AND YOUTH

Copyright © 1992 by Abingdon Press

The handouts in this book may be reprinted for use in the classroom in the local church or in the home, provided the following copyright notice is included: From *New Ways to Tell the Old, Old Story* by Delia Halverson. Copyright © 1992 by Abingdon Press. Reprinted by permission.

All rights reserved.
Other than the uses stated above, no part of this work may be reproduced or transmitted in any form or by any means, electronic or mechanical, including photocopying and recording, or by any information storage or retrieval system, except as may be expressly permitted by the 1976 Copyright Act or in writing from the publisher. Requests for permission should be addressed in writing to Abingdon Press, 201 Eighth Avenue South, Nashville, TN 37203.

This book is printed on recycled, acid-free paper.

Library of Congress Cataloging-in-Publication Data

HALVERSON, DELIA TOUCHTON.
 New ways to tell the old, old story : choosing and using Bible stories with children and youth / Delia Halverson.
  p. cm.
 Includes bibliographical references and index.
 ISBN 0-687-27946-1 (alk. paper)
 1. Bible stories—Study and teaching. I. Title.
BS546.H35   1992
220.9′505—dc20   91-36878
                                                              CIP

Scripture quotations, except for paraphrases or unless otherwise noted, are from the Revised Standard Version of the Bible, copyright 1946, 1952, 1971, or the New Revised Standard Version of the Bible, copyright © 1989, by the Division of Christian Education of the National Council of Churches of Christ in the United States of America and are used by permission.

Scripture noted GNB is from the *Good News Bible*—Old Testament: Copyright © American Bible Society 1976; New Testament: Copyright © American Bible Society 1966, 1971, 1976.

Scripture noted NIV is taken from the *Holy Bible: New International Version.* Copyright © 1973, 1978, 1984 by the International Bible Society. Used by permission of Zondervan Bible Publishers.

MANUFACTURED IN THE UNITED STATES OF AMERICA

To all the Sunday school teachers and youth program workers in the many churches across the country who share the joy of God's story with children and youth each week. And to the parents who are recognizing their role as Christian educators in the home. You are in my prayers.

Contents

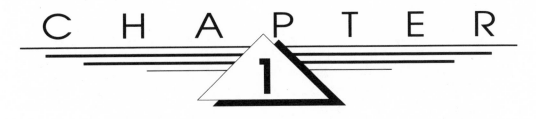

Why Teach Bible Stories to Children and Youth?

"Go on, Granddad. Read the next part of the story!" The young girl bounced up and down beside the older gentleman as they enjoyed the creation story together.

He reached out and placed his arm around her. "Why do you want to hear more?" he asked.

"I just can hardly wait to hear what our God will do next!"

Young children have a natural sense of excitement about the stories of the Bible. It is important to impress that enthusiasm in young children and to create excitement in older children and youth.

Excitement of this sort is caught rather than taught, unless of course the teaching is very creative and experiential. Then excitement is caught along with being taught. We retain very little of what we hear, more of what we both see and hear, and still more of what we experience. This is true for children and youth even more than for adults. And so, if we want our children and youth to get excited about the Bible, we must make it a part of their experience.

Giving Children and Youth Ownership in the Bible

The Bible was actually written as an adult book, although most of the stories were first told orally, probably in intergenerational groupings. This does not mean that children and youth cannot enjoy many of the stories. By surrounding our children and youth with the great stories of our biblical heritage, we help them claim the book as their own. We begin by telling the story in very simple words and holding the Bible on our laps. As reading skills grow, children read more for themselves. In teen years they can build research skills and use the Bible as a tool for their own personal faith.

Anyone who has worked with children and youth recognizes that the developmental pattern of each one is different. Recently I heard a news report stating that as adults turn forty-five they become interested in, of all things, buying new carpet. The person hosting the news show then asked, "Does that mean that on my forty-fifth birthday I am going to have a burning desire to run out and purchase a new carpet?" Of course it is not so cut-and-dried as that. And it is even more true that we cannot make blanket statements about children's abilities at specific ages. However, in this book when I use the term "young children" I am generally referring to preschool and early elementary. When I speak of "very young children" I have in mind primarily children who are pre-kindergarten.

It is important to keep in mind that the developmental progress of children varies, not only by age but also by cultural situation.

This was brought home to my attention when our daughter was taking reading readiness tests. To introduce the sound of the letter "G," the test used a picture of a swinging garden gate with a trellis over it. The picture was completely foreign to our daughter, whose primary experience with gates had been gates in barbed wire fences in South Dakota.

Young children seldom see the relationship of a Bible story to their own lives, because abstract thinking at those ages is not well developed. However, they can appreciate as good stories some of the stories that we adults hold important. As abstract thinking develops, we continue to use the stories. Repeating them over and over, we give essential but indirect guidance.

For a very young child, the story of the good shepherd may simply be a nice story about sheep. And we tell it that way, recognizing that the child's abstract thinking is not developed. But later, perhaps when the child has had an experience of feeling lost, the sense of joy over being found and the joy in the story will begin to click. An understanding unfolds in the child, based on the story learned earlier. The child experiences now and labels later.

The Bible Mandates Passing on the Faith

Scriptures from the early Hebrew tradition, stress learning God's word. In Deuteronomy (6:6-7), God commands us "And these words which I command you this day shall be upon your heart; and you shall teach them diligently to your children, and shall talk of them when you sit in your house, and when you walk by the way, and when you lie down, and when you rise."

The Hebrew people were very diligent about keeping the commandments. In fact, the leaders of Jesus' day were so concerned with the letter of the law that they forgot the real reason for study of the Scriptures. Jesus corrected such thoughts, and Paul tells us in II Timothy 3:16-17:

All scripture is inspired by God and is useful for teaching, for reproof, for correction, and for training in righteousness, so that everyone who belongs to God may be proficient, equipped for every good work.

We most often interpret this passage as instruction to use Scripture for inspiration or for knowledge of the Bible, or even for proving our personal beliefs. We ignore the latter part of the passage, which gives the real reason for studying the Scripture, "so that everyone who belongs to God may be proficient, equipped for every good work."

And so, why do we study Scripture? We should not study just for the sake of studying, or just in defense of our beliefs. Rather, we study Scripture to prepare ourselves to be God's disciples, to touch others' lives with God's love.

Giving Guidance in a Non-threatening Way

It is important to look at the theological concepts in a story before using it with children. The purpose for using a story may not be the same for children as for adults. Bible stories can give guidance as we enjoy the story. For example, the story of the boy who shared his lunch with Jesus and the multitude can help a child or a youth recognize the importance of sharing with others. Young children, of course, cannot grasp the full meaning of a miracle because they do not understand how the laws of nature render a miracle miraculous.

A Bible story about a child is not necessarily for a child. I would never tell the Isaac story (Genesis 22:1-19) to a young child. In the first place, the reasons for the Isaac story are all adult concepts. Abraham exhibited great trust in God and was dedicated to following what he believed God requested him to do. Young children have difficulty trusting anything they do not see. As they build their trust in their parents, the foundation is being laid for future understanding of God. By telling the story of Abraham's plan to sacrifice Isaac, we only diminish that trust in parents, weakening the link between loving parents and our loving God.

There is another reason the Isaac story has been recorded in our Bible. It pertains to cultural background. In that time in history, the Hebrews were living among pagan religions where child sacrifice was accepted, even expected. The telling of the story over and over affirmed to the people that their God was not one who demanded child sacrifice. In fact, in the story, God told Abraham to substitute the ram for the child.

More promising than a story *about* a child is the experience in a story that might be familiar *to* the child. In the story of Zacchaeus, the child can understand what it is like to be small and not able to see over the crowd. And what child doesn't love to climb a tree! Youth know what it is like to believe that you have no friends, that everyone is against you. Because children and youth can identify with the feelings and experiences of Zacchaeus, the story takes on new meaning. In so doing, it offers guidance.

Children Learn of Our Encounter with God Through Stories

Although children do not realize it as they first hear Bible stories, the stories begin to lay the foundation for becoming effective disciples of Christ.

The early Old Testament characters seemed to have a very close relationship with God. Abraham walked and talked with God in a very personal way. Jacob even wrestled with God. But after many generations of living in the community of foreign beliefs, the Israelites began to look on God as impersonal. In fact, when God spoke to Moses through the burning bush, Moses did not believe it. When Moses asked who God was, the answer came, "I am who I am." Moses insisted that God give him some sort of sign, because he knew that the people would not believe that he had spoken to God.

As the years passed and the people wandered through the wilderness, God cared for them. Yet they were still not convinced that God was interested in them personally. God finally gave them something more concrete, the Ten Commandments, in stone. And once they had this, they had to have an ark in which to place the commandments. This led to the tabernacle tent, and eventually to a temple, all in an effort to bring God into reality as the idea of God evolved. In I Samuel 8:7, we find God telling Samuel, "They have rejected me from being king over them." God must have been sad. God loves with a happy heart, and God loves with a sad heart, but God continues to love, even when we reject God. The people could not understand how to depend on God for their leadership. They wanted an earthly king, someone who would tell them just what to do.

When the Israelites were taken into exile, they felt separated from God. Even when the prophets told them that God was with them, they could not understand a personal God who would be with them wherever they went. On return from exile, they rebuilt the Temple, and every devout Hebrew made a yearly pilgrimage visit. The ark, where they believed God dwelt, was placed in the Holy of Holies, in the center of the Temple, where only the highest priest was allowed once a year.

And finally, God made God's self truly personal, through the life of Christ. When Jesus died, the ripping of the Temple veil that separated the Holy of Holies was symbolic of restoring our personal relationship with God. God was released, no longer curtained from the people. Jesus restored our relationship and gave us new insights. Through Jesus, we not only learn more about God, but because God had a human experience on earth, our relationship can be more personal than ever before.

Children and youth cannot grasp the full historical sweep of this story of our evolving concept of God. But as we supply bits of the story here and there, it begins to take shape. They can see God at work through people.

C H A P T E R

2

Guidelines
for Selecting Bible Stories

As we consider specific stories for certain age groups, we need to recognize the levels of perception and skill of the children and youth. One of the primary factors to consider is the ability to think abstractly. When our son was five, one of his friends asked, "What is the word that is something like a million?" Another friend said, "You mean a dozen?" The first responded with excitement, "Yeah, there were a dozen of them!" Young children bring this same sort of understanding to the story of Jesus feeding the multitude. They can, however, appreciate the fact that Jesus cared when the people were hungry, and that there was a boy in the crowd who shared.

In all miracle stories shared with young children, we need to emphasize the caring aspect of Jesus. We certainly want to help both children and youth realize that miracles are different from magic. Magic is built on illusions.

Next, let's look at the stories themselves. We need not feel that a child or a youth must be familiar with every story in the Bible, but there are basic stories that we hope they will know by the time they reach adulthood.

Your church may have a curriculum goal that includes a specific list of stories. If not, consider the list below. Of course, each child is different, and you need to seriously consider each situation. If a story is introduced when it relates to a current life experience, then the story has more meaning.

Specific Ages to Introduce Suggested Stories

Younger Preschool

Old Testament:
God Made the World (Genesis 1:1, 27, 31)

New Testament:
Birth of Jesus (Luke 2:1-7)
Shepherds Hear the Good News (Luke 2:8-20)
Jesus Grew and Helped Joseph (Luke 2:39-40)
A Boy Shares His Lunch of Loaves and Fishes (John 6:1-14)
Jesus Helps Jairus' Daughter (Luke 8:40-42, 49-56)

(New Testament cont.)
Zacchaeus (Luke 19:1-10)
Jesus Loves the Children (Luke 18:15-17)
Jesus Rides into Jerusalem (Mark 11:1-11)
Jesus' Last Supper (Matthew 26:17-20, 26-28; Mark 14:17-25; Luke 22:14-38)
Jesus' Enemies Killed Him, but God Didn't Let Jesus Stay Dead (treated together in simple form—Matthew 27:35a, 57-60; 28:1-8)
Jesus Has a Cookout with His Friends (omitting when it happened—John 21:1-13)

Older Preschool

Old Testament:

The Big Flood (Genesis 6:14, 19-22, 7:17, 8:1-20, 9:13-15)
(Do not emphasize the sinfulness of the world here. Older preschoolers' abstract thinking is not advanced enough.)
Abraham's Faithful Journey (Genesis 12:1-5)
Miriam Cares for Her Brother (Exodus 2:1-10)
Ruth Is Kind to Her Mother-in-Law (Ruth 2)
Samuel Helps Eli (I Samuel 2:18)
Solomon Builds the Temple (I Kings 5–8, selected)

New Testament:

Mary's Promise of a Child (Luke 1:26-38) (Ignore the virginity of Mary. Older preschoolers are too young to understand.)
Visit of the Wise Men (Matthew 2:1-2, 9-11)
Presentation of Baby Jesus at the Temple (Luke 2:22-39)
Jesus Teaches in the Synagogue (Luke 4:14-30)
Jesus Calms the Storm (Mark 4:35-41)
Jesus' Story of the Lost Sheep (Luke 15:3-7)
One of Ten Tells Jesus Thank You (Luke 17:11-19)
The Birthday of the Church (Acts 1:4, 5, 13-14, 2:1-17, 22-47)

Younger Elementary

Old Testament:

Creation (Genesis 1:1–2:3)
Tower of Babel (Genesis 11:1-9)
Isaac Is Born (Genesis 21:1-7)
Moses and the Wanderings (Exodus 1–20, selected)
Battle of Jericho (Joshua 6:1-20)
God Calls Samuel (I Samuel 3:1-10, 19-20)
David and Goliath (I Samuel 17:1-58)
David and Jonathan (I Samuel 19–20, selected)
A Woman and Her Son Care for Elijah (I Kings 17:8-15)
The Boy, Jeremiah, Answers God (Jeremiah 1:4-8)

New Testament:

Escape with Baby Jesus to Egypt (Matthew 2:13-23)
Jesus as a Boy in the Temple (Luke 2:41-52)
John the Baptist Tells of Jesus' Coming (Matthew 3:1-12)
Jesus' Baptism (Matthew 3:13-17)
Jesus' Temptation (Luke 4:1-15)

(New Testament cont.)

Jesus Invites Friends to Follow Him (Luke 5:1-11; Matthew 9:35–10:8)
Jesus Attends a Wedding (John 2:1-12)
Friends Bring to Jesus a Man Who Cannot Walk (Mark 2:1-12)
Jesus Heals a Lame Man at the Pool (John 5:1-15)
Parable of Good Samaritan (Luke 10:25-37)
Jesus' Friends, Mary and Martha (Luke 10:38-42)
Jesus Teaches About Prayer (Luke 11:1-4; Matthew 6:7-15)
Parable of the Forgiving Father (Luke 15:11-32)
Jesus Heals a Deaf Man (Mark 7:31-37)
Jesus and the Moneychangers (John 2:13-22)
The Resurrection (Matthew 28:1-10; Luke 24:1-12; John 20:1-18)
Philip Tells of Jesus (Acts 8:26-40)
The Road to Damascus (Acts 9:1-25)
Lydia, the Businesswoman (Acts 16:11-15)
An Earthquake at the Jail (Acts 16:16-40)

Older Elementary

Old Testament:

The Garden of Eden (Genesis 3)

God's Covenant with Noah (Genesis 6:5–9:17)

Esau and Jacob (Genesis 25:20-34; 32:3-21; 33:1-4)

Joseph (Genesis 37–47)

Deborah, the Judge and Prophetess (Judges 4:4-23)

Ruth and Naomi (Ruth)

King David (I and II Samuel, selected)

Elijah and the Prophets of Baal (I Kings 18:1, 17-45)

Queen Esther (Esther)

Daniel in the Lions' Den (Daniel 6)

Jonah Runs from God (Jonah)

New Testament:

Birth of John the Baptist (Luke 1:5-25, 57-76)

Disciples Pick Grain on the Sabbath (Mark 2:23-28)

(New Testament cont.)

Parable of the Sower (Matthew 13:1-9, 18-23)

Jesus Walks on Water (Matthew 14:22-33)

Two Men Praying in the Temple (Luke 18:9-14)

Lazarus (John 11:1-44)

Parable of Servants' Use of Money (Matthew 25:14-30)

A Woman Who Washed Jesus' Feet (Luke 7:36-50)

Last Supper, Gethsemane, Trial, Crucifixion (Matthew 26:14–27:66)

Thomas Finally Believes (John 20:19-29)

Friends Traveling to Emmaus (Luke 24:13-35)

Stephen, the First Christian Martyr (Acts 6:8–8:1)

Peter Escapes from Jail (Acts 12:1-19)

Paul's Missionary Journeys (Acts 13–28)

Middle School

Old Testament:

Two Creation Stories (Genesis 1:1–2:25)

God's Covenant with Abraham (Genesis 12–15)

Abraham Obeys God (Genesis 22:1-19) (Note: "Obeys" is more affirmative than Abraham's "testing.")

Babylonian Exile (II Chronicles, selected)

Valley of Dry Bones (Ezekiel 37:1-14)

New Testament:

Kingdom of God Is Like a Mustard Seed (Mark 4:30-34)

Jesus Sends His Followers Out to Teach (Luke 10:1-12, 16-20)

(New Testament cont.)

Parable of the Unmerciful Servant (Matthew 18:23-35)

Parable of Workers in the Vineyard (Matthew 20:1-16)

Parable of Two Sons (Matthew 21:28-31)

Parable of Invitations to a Wedding (Matthew 22:1-10; Luke 14:15-24)

Transfiguration of Jesus (Luke 9:28-36)

The Widow's Gift (Mark 12:41-44)

I Was Hungry and You Fed Me (Matthew 25:31-46)

Jesus Taken Up into Heaven (Acts 1:1-11)

Peter Heals a Man (Acts 3:1-10)

High School

Old Testament:

Rahab's Story (Joshua 2:1-24, 6:1-25)

Abigail Helps David (I Samuel 25, 27:2-3, 30:1-6, 18)

Elijah and the Chariots of Fire (II Kings 2:1-15)

A Good Man Has Problems (Job)

New Testament:

Jesus Tells of a Dinner Party (Luke 14:1, 7-14)

Parable of the Persistent Widow (Luke 18:1-8)

Parable of Ten Women with Lamps (Matthew 25:1-13)

Jesus' Death (Luke 23:26-47)

The Holy City (Revelation 21)

Age Level Goals for Studying the Bible

AGE LEVEL	GOALS FOR STUDENTS (to know or accomplish)	GOALS FOR TEACHER
Preschool	Learn that the Bible tells us about God and Jesus.	Hold the Bible while telling the stories. Use markers for simple verses.
1st Grade	Learn that the Old Testament was written before the time of Jesus and contains the scriptures that he read. Learn that the New Testament tells about Jesus and those who spread the message of Jesus after his death and resurrection. Become familiar with some of the names of the books of the Bible and of persons in the Bible. By the end of the year, begin to learn the names of the Gospels and that "gospel" means "Good News."	Read short stories from the Bible.
2nd Grade	Read Bible story in part and learn key words. Learn about customs, dress, and food of Bible days. Become familiar with the Bible's table of contents. Use bookmarks that teacher has placed in Bible ahead of time.	Tell a Bible story and then allow children to read it in part. Create biblical atmosphere. Place bookmarks in Bible for student use.
3rd Grade	Begin to associate books with sections of Bible. Learn beginning skills: book, chapter, verse, abbreviation of books.	Identify Bible sections when speaking of specific books.
4th Grade	Learn to use a children's Bible dictionary. Frequently practice skills of locating scripture.	Give reference locations often. Be aware of varying reading skills.

Age Level Goals for Studying the Bible (cont'd)

AGE LEVEL	GOALS FOR STUDENTS (to know or accomplish)	GOALS FOR TEACHER
5th, 6th Grade	Locate the books of the Bible according to category. Use maps with Bible study. Learn about historical development of the Bible. Memorize books of the Bible.	Encourage using Bible for personal enrichment. Introduce several Bible translations briefly. Emphasize that it is more important to be able to locate the scripture passage than to be able to recite books in order.
7th, 8th Grade	Compare different Gospel writers' versions of the same story. Use footnotes/cross-references in the Bible.	Recommend scriptures for personal reading.
Senior High	Use concordance to locate references on a specific theme.	Introduce comprehensive Bible dictionaries.
Adult	Become familiar with Bible translations (versions that observe strict scholarly rules and stay close to original text) and paraphrases (versions that freely add interpretative materials to original text). Use commentaries.	Provide Bible reference materials in classroom.

In considering which stories are most appropriate for specific ages and which stories might be appropriate for particular children or youth, consider not only the religious content and the moral teaching, but also the emotional effect on the children. Be aware of what is happening in their lives at any point. Chapter 4 will help you relate specific stories to life situations of children and youth.

Young children love action stories. Many of the stories can emphasize the action. In her book *When Jesus Was Born*, Mary Ann Dotts retells the Advent story emphasizing words, sounds, actions, and feelings. Each page has one word, repeated three times, and a picture along with a few brief lines of story. Soon the child is able to tell the story by looking at the pictures and using the repeated words.

The Old Testament is filled with action stories, yet not all action stories in the Bible are appropriate for young children. When selecting Old Testament stories, look for positive acts on the part of the characters, particularly positive acts toward any children in the story. Boaz shared his field of grain with Ruth, and she gathered grain to share with Naomi. The rooftop room was prepared by the family to welcome Elisha. Miriam cared for the infant Moses.

When using the Moses story with young children, emphasize the care that Miriam gave her baby brother by watching him and arranging with the princess to bring her mother to care for him. With young children, the story of Noah should center on how he built the ark and cared for the animals during the Flood. God's destruction of the world with the flood is a concept for older children, as is the concept of the covenant.

I have already mentioned the Isaac story, which I would avoid teaching young children (see p. 10). Parts of the Samuel story need to be treated with caution also. When we use the complete story of Samuel's childhood, a young child may fear being left by parents, as Samuel was left at the temple. This may be circumvented in a couple of ways. We can simply begin the story saying that Samuel was a boy who lived in the temple with Eli. He learned much about God from Eli and enjoyed talking to God. Or we may tell the story from the beginning, stating that in that time, in order to help in the temple, which was like our church, you had to live at the temple. But today we can live at home and still be helpers in the church.

Selecting Bible Story Books

I have personally had trouble finding Bible story books for very young children. Most editors seem to think that every story in the Bible should be covered in one book! Consequently, most books contain stories inappropriate for children younger than three or four, or even as old as six. I like to save stories from curriculum leaflets and make my own storybooks for young children.

As you consider a book for a specific-age child, look at the wording. The words of a book that you will read to a pre-reader may be more difficult than those in a book for beginning readers. The beginning reader may understand many words, but he or she will have a very limited reading vocabulary. Most new books will suggest an age span. Again, however, you must consider the individual child or children. What the editor considers average may not be average for your community or family. Or you may find that the concepts in a book are too abstract for the age level.

I prefer books that simply tell the story to books that tack on a moral at the end of the story. If the moral in the story is appropriate for the child, then the child will likely grasp that concept without its having to be called to his or her attention. And if the concept is too sophisticated for the child, then the story simply becomes a nice narrative. The child will not understand the moral even if he or she repeats it after you.

When a book includes a multitude of questions to "test" how well the child listened, I find that the questions are often meaningless or inappropriate for specific children. I have found a few books that have questions that engage the children in the story, such as *Moses and the Great Escape* by Tim Dowley. This book, with detailed illustrations, asks questions about the illustrations that draw the reader (child or adult) into the action of the story. Often, however, books with questions at the end of the story have weak story plots. The story should engage the reader for the joy of the story, not to answer the questions.

One of my favorite kinds of Bible story books, for all ages, is the might-have-been story. Since the Bible is actually an adult book, might-have-been stories can be written on the child's level. They usually help to bring out the everyday reality of the story. These stories have taken the point of view of a person who might have lived during the time of the story and might have been an observer of the action. When using these stories, be sure to state that they are might-have-been stories—stories that someone imagines might have happened. *The Pail of Nails* by Harriet May Savitz and K. Michael Syring is a good example of this type of book.

The pictures in a Bible story book are of primary importance. They should reflect the times and the event accurately. They should stimulate thought about the story and communicate the message. With our vivid video world of today, children are accustomed to colorful pictures. Color is important, although well-done simple black-and-white drawings can be effective.

For young children, look for pictures that focus on the action; avoid too much clutter. Older children can appreciate more detail. Peter Spier's *Noah's Ark* has delightful detail. In fact, the whole story is told in pictures, down to the hash marks on the wall of the ark indicating the days of the Flood and the smile on the cow's face as she eats the olive branch that the dove brought back.

Pictures for young children should not depict brutality, even if that was a part of the story. I have been known to tear out of a book the picture of Solomon, poised with a sword above the child as he tries to determine the real mother. No picture in a Bible story book should frighten a child. Editors are wise not to use pictures of the more violent episodes from our Bible heritage. Without seeing the picture, children can usually regulate the degree of violence that they can handle. The way a child reacts to a story often depends on the storyteller. The greater the trust, the more variety of material the storyteller can narrate.

Bible Translations and Reference Tools

I recommend Bible story books for first- and second-grade reading. You will, however, want to locate short scripture passages for beginning readers to read on their own. Of course it is important, even with preschool children, to hold a Bible on your lap when you tell the story, or to have one nearby that you pick up when you explain that the story comes from the Bible. I like to highlight a verse in the story or the name of the character in the story and put a corresponding marker in the Bible, then to encourage the preschooler to open the Bible to the marker and tell the story himself or herself. The beginning reader can recognize the character's name. Better readers in these grades might use the *International Children's Version* mentioned below. The American Bible Society also puts out sections of the New Testament in a Translation for Early Youth. The Bible Society's new Contemporary English Version of the New Testament, *Bible for Today's Family*, is also available. The entire Bible is scheduled for publication in 1996.

When we begin looking at Bibles for readers, it is important to recognize the difference between a translation and a paraphrase. Translations follow strict scholarly rules and stay close to the original text. The *International Children's Version* of the New Testament is written on a third-grade level and is easy to read. It has definitions of some words at the bottom of the page; however, it is not appropriate for learning the skill of finding chapter and verse references in the Bible because it is not so marked. The *Good*

News Bible is appropriate for third and fourth graders as they improve their Bible skills.

Older elementary and youth enjoy the *Good News Bible*. Look for cross-references, word lists, short introductions for each book, outlines of books, footnotes, and good illustrations and maps. Youth can also use the *New International Version* and the Revised or New Revised Standard Version. You may want to check the curriculum materials used by your church and select the translation most often used there.

The *New English Bible* is especially readable in the Old Testament, but it generally reflects British idiom, because it was translated in England.

The King James Version is a masterpiece of older English prose. People who learned scripture from the KJV feel very comfortable with it. However, much of the language is not compatible with what our children know today. Youth and older elementary children can appreciate it more if they realize that the "thee's" and "thou's" were common at the time it was translated, but were very personal, used for close family and loved ones. "You" and "your" were formal words, used to address royalty. Today we have completely reversed the usage. When students understand this bit of history, the words in the King James Version will seem more loving and more personal.

A paraphrase adds interpretative materials to the original text. For general reading, this is enjoyable and can help hold the reader's interest. It is important to emphasize, however, that someone has *added* words to the Bible. One of my favorite paraphrases is J. B. Phillips' *New Testament*.

For suggestions and ideas about Bible presentations in the church, I refer you to Pat Griggs' book, *Opening the Bible with Children*. The book also contains good suggestions for beginning Bible skills.

Encourage older elementary children and youth to own a "working Bible" that they can highlight, underline, and use to write in the margins. This will need to have a strong binding and wide margins for notes. The pages should be heavy enough that the writing does not show through on the other side. Maps and pictures are helpful, and extra background information at the beginning of each book and elsewhere in the Bible is important.

Middle schoolers and high schoolers can begin using additional reference books. A Bible dictionary gives brief descriptions of various words, such as Herod, harlot, bed, and money. This helps not only with vocabulary but also with gaining historical background.

Some Bibles have selective concordances, which include the key or most important words. A complete concordance will include every word that is used in the Bible, listing every location for the word. This helps when you know parts of a verse but cannot locate it. It also helps you locate scriptures on the same subject.

Bible commentaries are published in both one-volume editions and multi-volume editions. Most church libraries have these. They give the writer's viewpoint about particular passages. Some "study Bibles" have commentary written alongside the scripture. I personally prefer to have the commentary in a separate book so that I do my own thinking about the text before I go to someone else's views. A new series, *A Storyteller's Companion*, edited by Michael E. Williams (Abingdon), is helpful for a teacher's background study. High school classes can appreciate the stories and use it as a resource. The series covers individual books and groups of books in the Old Testament.

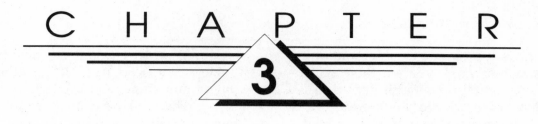

Adapting Curriculum Materials

As you read and begin to recognize that I have included many experiential activities for teaching Bible stories, you may question just why we need to use curriculum at all.

Bible stories are a part of our Christian heritage, and we are eager for our children and youth to learn them. However, we must remember that the goal of teaching Bible stories is to help children develop their own relationship with God and live out God's call for their lives.

Most published curriculum has a specific plan that introduces the student to the principal Bible stories several times during childhood and youth years, using the stories in ways appropriate to their ages. Your church could, of course, devise your own goals and curriculum. However, this is not only time-consuming, but you must also be certain that you are using activities and materials appropriate to each age. If you do not adopt some sort of curriculum plan, whether devised in the local church or published, there is a chance that teachers will tend to use only their favorite Bible stories. Then you may find that the same favorite stories are repeated over and over, and the students are not exposed to other important stories.

During our children's elementary and teen years, our family made several moves about the country. When we attended the same denominational church, it was good to know that our children were in a continuing program of curriculum. We knew that the plan was well thought through and that the children would not miss important learnings as they changed churches. This is a plus for our mobile society today. It is also a plus for children who spend alternate weekends with parents after a divorce.

Another advantage is that published curriculum has individual student pieces that can be taken home, allowing the parents to expand the learning during the week.

Published curriculum is either life-centered or Bible-centered. Life-centered curriculum does not ignore the Bible, but rather it uses scripture in the learning process. A life-centered curriculum gives good entry points, particularly for families who are new to Christianity.

It is important that much of the curriculum be life-centered, particularly as the student reaches older elementary and teen years. These are the years when the students are anxious about what is going on in their lives. Their peers are of prime importance, and they are beginning to make more and more decisions on their own. It is in these years that we want the Bible to become a guide for living, not just a book of great stories. Teens will not use it as a guide for daily decision making unless they recognize where and how it can be beneficial to them. With life-centered curriculum, their interest is captured immediately. They see that it is important for them.

Curriculum is usually written with more activities than most classes can accomplish in the allotted time. Consequently, you will need to make choices. You may also find that certain activities simply are not suitable for your class and you will want to plan a substitution. Some of the activities in this book may be substitutes. It is important that you read the goals of your session and be certain, when you do substitute, that your alternate activity carries out those goals.

If you do alter your lesson plan, I suggest that you follow the guidelines Dorothy Jean Furnish suggests in her book *Experiencing the Bible with Children* (Nashville: Abingdon Press, 1990, pp. 74-80):

One bridge between past and present is that people in both worlds share similar emotions . . . *The first guideline, then, in helping children experience the Bible, is to enable them to "feel into" the text.* When they can feel the same emotions as those felt by the persons in the story, they are well on their way to understanding the story itself. . . . Any activity that can help children express emotion is a good "feeling into" activity. . . .

The second guideline is to help children "meet with" the text in an exciting and involving way. The "meeting with" is the planting of the seed into the soil that has been prepared with "feeling into" activities. . . . The most appropriate methods for "meeting with" are those that are most likely to stimulate the child to say, "It feels as if I am really there!" . . .

The third guideline, then, in helping children experience the Bible is to encourage them to "respond out of" their encounter with the Bible text. . . . This response may be likened to the harvest that follows the planting of the seed in the prepared soil.

The teacher's task is to provide the classroom climate for a positive response. This may mean simply hearing and accepting the spontaneous comments or unspoken responses. . . . It may mean making plans that will draw out or help children express what they feel but have not said. It will also suggest that you, as teacher or parent, share what the text means to you, since the exchange is an important part of teaching.

For an example of Furnish's guidelines, as you teach the story of Jesus healing the blind man who sat by the side of the road (Luke 18:35-42), you might use these methods:

Feeling Into: Pair up the students for a trust walk. Blindfold one out of each pair, and have the other student lead the blindfolded student on a short walk. Then reverse the situation so that each student has opportunity to "feel into" the experience of living without sight.

Meeting With: Following the directions for a story web in chapter 11 (page 71), have the students read sections of the story. A story as short as this one may be repeated, with different students actively participating. Children respond to a repetition in order for all students to have a part, and the repetition reinforces the story.

Responding Out Of: The students may devise a story walk (see chapter 12, page 73) for the story. This is done on paper footprints, which may then be placed in the hallway where adults, as well as children and youth, can enjoy the result.

If you find that your students especially enjoy a particular learning method you might expand the method and use it throughout the session. For example, if your students enjoy poetry and you are studying Jesus as a boy in the Temple (Luke 2:41-52), begin with a "feeling into" experience by asking them to write a cinquain poem (see chapter 7, page 47) about losing a loved one in a crowd. Then to "meet with" the story, use a poem litany (see chapter 11, page 68), such as this:

The Boy Jesus in the Temple

Leader: Each year the parents of Jesus went to Jerusalem.

All: For a Passover Feast!

Leader: When Jesus was twelve, he was excited to be going along.

All: He wanted to talk to priests!

Group 1: There was singing and feasting . . .

Group 2: With old friends and new.

All: And Jesus talked with scholars and priests.

Leader: When the time came to leave, families traveled together,

Group 1: And the children ran from group to group.

Leader: But as night came upon them, Jesus was not to be found,

Group 2: Not with aunts or cousins or friends.

Leader: Jesus' parents turned back. Just where could they find him?

All: The second day they searched and searched.

Leader: On the third day they found him, with priests in the Temple.

All: He amazed those who heard him with intelligent answers.

Leader: But his mother wondered and asked:

Girl: "Son, why have you done this?
We've worried and searched.
    Why did you stay behind?"

Leader: And Jesus quite calmly gave her his answer:

Boy: "Did you not know me enough?
You need not have worried.
My Father's house is where I must be."

Leader: Then Jesus went with them—back to Nazareth,

Voice 1: And he grew in wisdom . . .

Voice 2: And in body . . .

All: And in favor with God and with men.

You may plan for the class to "respond out of" the story by using the shape of a temple building to make a picture poem of the story. (See chapter 7, page 46.)

Another example of adapting an activity to fulfill more than one guideline can be found in chapter 6, page 35, using creative movement.

From the time I first discovered Dorothy Furnish's guidelines, they have been a model for my teaching, and I have used them in curriculum writing. Her book *Experiencing the Bible with Children* will help you learn to identify methods to use for each of the guidelines. She also gives guidance in helping children answer the question "What does it mean to me?" I highly recommend that you enrich your teaching with this book.

As you work with these guidelines, take special care not to let your activities fall into just one category. The real learning comes as the student meets the story in all three areas. And, of course, remember to consider the age appropriateness of all your activities.

4

Weaving Everyday Experiences into Bible Stories

The classroom experience and everyday life are often helpful when telling Bible stories. As you tell a story you may make reference to such experiences, or you may start from the experience, using it as a springboard for telling a Bible story.

Become saturated with the stories, so that when an opportunity to share one springs up, you are prepared. You will want to sharpen your storytelling skills in order to make the telling spontaneous.

Spontaneous Experiences

When you are waiting for a meal and you are all hungry, remind everyone that those who listened to Jesus on the hillside must have been hungry before he multiplied the fish and loaves. This "feeling into" experience can be as simple as saying, "I'm as hungry as the people on the hillside must have been before Jesus fed them the loaves and the fish." If they are familiar with the story, then the simple reminder has brought it into their everyday experience. If it is not a familiar story, then tell the story simply. After a filling meal, where you have plenty of food left, you might lead into the story by saying, "This must be how the people felt after Jesus fed the multitude" (John 6:1-14).

Snack time with young children is an ideal time for telling stories of Jesus eating with his disciples. Don't forget one of my favorites, the time that Jesus had a cook-out with his disciples (John 21:1-14). You might also use stories such as the Passover meal in Egypt (Exodus 12), the quail and manna from heaven (Exodus 16), the Feast of Tabernacles (Leviticus 23:33-43), Boaz giving Ruth grain (Ruth 2), or Mary and Martha (Luke 10:38-42).

Headline News

As you read the newspaper or hear news reports, be aware of opportunities to parallel Bible stories to news events. Most older elementary and teens can relate to this.

A newsstory about someone who broke the law because he or she felt it was the caring thing to do might spearhead a discussion on Exodus 20:8-11, 31:12-17; Mark 3:1-5; and Luke 14:1-6. A story about feeding hungry refugees might lead to a discussion of Jesus' feeding the multitude (John 6:1-15) or a discussion of Matthew 25:31-46, when the king said, "I was hungry . . ." The story of Jesus' reaction to the woman who was caught in adultery (John 8:1-11) might come out of a newsstory about a criminal being given a light sentence. Most such discussions are used to "respond out of" the story.

Create Experiences

Look for times you might create opportunities to weave life experiences into Bible stories. With older elementary and youth you might set up this "feeling into" situation for discussion of Genesis 3. Place a bowl of popcorn in the room, and, before the session, privately tell a student of your plan and ask him or her to talk the others into taking some popcorn while you are out of the room, convincing them that no one will know. During the session find an excuse to leave the room and ask the students not to eat any of the popcorn. While you are out, the clued-in student will act as the "serpent," persuading them to disobey. When you return, ask who took the popcorn. The students will point to the "serpent." It is important, as you select the person to help you in this sort of situation, that it is someone whose self-esteem will not be injured when he or she is blamed for the "sin." It will also be more effective if it isn't someone who is likely to do such a thing without prompting.

The parable of sowing the seeds (Matthew 13:1-9) will be more real if you find a place to actually plant seeds in various soil, light, and water conditions, and then watch the results. This "responding out of" experience can extend for weeks. Young children cannot understand the abstract connection between the growth of seeds and Jesus' words, but they will have an experience with the parable that they can build on later.

A trust walk, where you pair up students and one is blindfolded and the other must lead, will give the students a "feeling into" experience to understand what it must be like to be blind. This can lead into any of the stories of Jesus healing someone who was blind (Luke 18:35-42).

You may want to create a covenant with your class about what you will provide for their use in the classroom and in turn, how they will care for the room and equipment. With elementary and teens, this can lead into a discussion about covenants in the Bible (Genesis 9:8-17; Genesis 15; Exodus 6:2-8; Luke 22:20; I Corinthians 11:23-26).

CHAPTER 5

Using Art Activities to Tell the Story

God created each of us unique. Consequently, we all learn in different ways and from different experiences. If we are going to teach children and youth our heritage stories, then we need to devise various methods of teaching so that each student can learn the story in a way that suits him or her best. Each teacher is also unique. You will find that some teaching methods are natural for you, and others are extremely difficult. It may be that some of these methods are more compatible to your teaching style than a particular one in your curriculum. It is legitimate to substitute. You will, of course, want to be sure that the purpose of the lesson is carried out through your substitute activities. Consider your students and yourself as you prepare to share Bible stories.

Young children are comfortable using art if we do not criticize. It is true that their work is far from perfect. In fact, that is why most of us, as adults, feel uncomfortable expressing ourselves through art. As children, we may have felt pressured to produce beautiful work and were therefore discouraged when we could not live up to adults' expectations. It is important to affirm all art work with students, no matter the age. Sometimes that affirmation comes simply by saying, "Tell me something about your picture. How did you feel as you were drawing it?" Accepting the student's

work, just the way it is, encourages creativity. In Christian education, we are not out to create artists. The pressure for perfection is off. We can leave the art teaching to the public schools and concentrate on the joy of creating as God made us to create. Our goal is to help the student create an *experience* with the story. We must remind ourselves that the "doing" is important, not the finished product.

Children and youth do take pride in their work, and it is important to display their work at times. Other times you will want to have them take the art projects home with them. One benefit of sending the art with them is that students can review the Bibles stories at home, where they live seven days a week. There is no need to keep most art work on display more than two or three weeks. When we remove it and send it home, the room takes on a new and exciting atmosphere as we put up new items. Students will wonder, "How will our room look this week?"

When planning to use an art activity, be sure that you first experiment with it yourself. This clears up any misunderstanding you may have about just how the activity is accomplished. Although each method suggested in this chapter has a list of supplies needed, you will be better prepared if you experiment. You will also create an example for students to see, and if you have the sort of talents that I have for art, your sample will show them that you are not seeking perfection!

As you work with children and youth on art activities, there are opportunities to expand on the background or meaning of the story. You might ask, "Have you ever seen a shepherd?" Or you might say, "How do you suppose the man in your picture felt when Jesus healed him?"

In these suggestions I have purposefully omitted using food for art activities. When we use food as a non-food item and later try to initiate concern for people who are hungry, we send mixed signals. On one hand, we tell the students that food is a non-essential and can be glued on paper, and on the other hand we tell them that food is important and should not be wasted because some people are starving. We want to teach Christ's way in everything that we do, and we are not teaching good stewardship of our resources when we use food in this way.

Clay

Often overlooked, clay gives opportunity for expression. It can be used to form figures to illustrate a Bible story, or it can be used to create feelings as you "feel into" the story. Young children particularly enjoy the feel of clay. As we get older we are more inhibited about using it, but with experimentation, all ages can appreciate clay. Teens will enjoy working with the clay as you tell or talk about the story.

Materials needed:
Clay or play dough (All homemade mixtures I have seen call for food items. I have used a cookie dough for modeling and then baked it into cookies. If you do this, be sure to stress cleanliness.)

Even young children can make their clay into a head and mold the eyes and nose and then make a happy or sad mouth, expressing how the leper felt when he went to see Jesus and how he felt after Jesus healed him, or how Jesus felt when the leper returned to thank him, and how he must have felt when he remembered that the other nine did not thank him (Luke 17:11-19).

Collage

A collage is a three-dimensional method of telling the story, using an assortment of items that are attached to a surface. The surface may be hung on a wall or laid flat. The story need not be depicted in detail, but rather use items or illustrations within the collage to remind us of parts of the story. In this way it may be used as a response activity after "meeting with" the story. You may want to use it as a "feeling into" activity, creating a collage that expresses how you feel about something. For example, dark items and a few bright spots arranged chaotically might depict how the disciples must have felt in the boat in the midst of the storm. Older children and youth can understand this, but the concept is too abstract for younger children. For their concrete minds, make an outline of the boat for them to construct with wood chips, and use pebbles for the shore (Mark 4:35-41).

A collage of pictures may also be made as an opportunity to review a whole quarter's Bible stories. You might use various curriculum pictures and place them at interesting angles on the surface. This is an effective way to make a cover for a book of Bible stories.

Materials needed:
For background or surface: cardboard or tops of boxes, construction paper, paper plates, pieces of wood, etc.
Collection of an assortment of items: egg shells, cotton balls, scraps of fur or leather, fabrics, straws, buttons, wood shavings, small stones, paper scraps, pictures, etc. (Note my reference above to the use of food.)
White glue or another strong glue

Give the students opportunity to explore the various materials you have provided. (If you plan ahead, you can ask students to bring materials to add to your supply.)

Talk about what you want to do with the collage. If you are simply retelling the story, talk about the scene you want to create and what might be used for parts of the picture. If you are creating symbols or suggestions of the story, talk about what symbols you might use. Remember that young children think concretely, and abstract symbols are often beyond their reach. You might use fabric for the clothing, cotton balls for sheep, pebbles or sand for the road, sandpaper for the buildings, and so on. If you create a collage to "feel into" the story, then talk about how the items remind you of those feelings.

Comic Books

Creating comic books is especially exciting for middle elementary children to "respond out of" the story. Scenes are drawn on uniform-size paper and then reduced in the copy machine and pasted together to form the sequence.

Materials needed:
Paper of uniform size; typing paper is best.
Pencils
Copy machine with reduction capability
Tape
Colored pencils or crayons (optional)

Plan as a group just what scenes will need to be used to make the story complete. Where possible, allow the students to choose the scenes they want to draw. Assign any scenes not chosen.

After all scenes are completed, reduce them and place in sequence. (See p. 28.) Make enough copies for each student to have a book. Collate and staple the pages together to form the comic book. Each student may color his or her book. Color one or two copies for the church library.

Drawing and Painting

Drawing and painting are the most common art activities, and we tend to overuse them primarily because they require so little preparation. When we create a picture in this way, we are actually putting a part of ourselves on the paper, and so as adults we need to be conscientious when we talk about the drawings or paintings. The best way to comment on a child's drawing is to ask him or her to tell about it first. This eliminates your mistakenly calling a donkey a camel!

Materials needed:
Paper (size depending on use)
Pencils, crayons, markers, chalk, tempera, watercolors, etc.

Give young children opportunity to choose their own expressions. You might suggest that they draw or paint the part of the Bible story that they liked best. Older children and youth may select specific parts of one story, so that when the drawings or paintings are complete you have told the whole story. For a sharing experience, collate and staple the pages together into a book and give it to a preschool class. Remember that we are not teaching drawing and painting; we are using them as a tool or method. If a student is having difficulty drawing, you might suggest ways that help us create, such as using circles for parts of the human body or ovals for fish or rectangles for buildings.

Graffiti Wall

A graffiti wall is one of my favorite introductory or "feeling into" activities. It may also be used to review a story.

Materials needed:
Large paper to place on wall
Markers or crayons

If you will be using markers, test the paper to be sure it will not bleed through on the

5. Michael D   Genesis 37:

6.

Joseph became
head person of
in charge of
Potiphar's house
but then he
was unfairly
put in prison

Erika Arnovitz
Genesis 40
8

The meaning
of Dreams

9. Michael D   Genesis 41:
The King's strange dream

7   Michael D

Genesis 39:
Joseph is
thrown into Prison

10.   Michael D   Genesis 41:
The King's dream

wall. If it does, double the paper or protect the wall in some way. Secure the paper to the wall.

Title the graffiti wall with the name of the story or print instructions, such as: Draw a picture or symbol, or use words to tell how you feel when someone calls you an unpleasant name.

Although the actual learning in this experience comes as the students make the wall, you will want to be certain that you also make reference to the graffiti wall later during the session.

Greeting Cards

Greeting cards can be used at any time of the year. Get well cards or "hello" cards are appropriate when your Bible story emphasizes caring for others. Nativity or Holy Week scenes may be drawn on Christmas or Easter cards. Older children and youth will enjoy making cards with symbols. Younger children may also make symbols, but they will appreciate them simply as symbols of the season rather than understand the religious meaning.

Materials needed:
Rectangular paper, folded in half and then in half again
Crayons, markers, watercolors, etc.
Envelope for mailing

Prepare the student by talking about why you are making the card and who will receive it. Unless they are to be sent in bulk to some place like a nursing home, it is best for the student to have in mind a particular person to whom a card will be sent. Encourage neatness, reminding the students that these are for someone else, but do not stifle creativity. Greeting cards make an excellent activity for "responding out of" the story.

Kiosk

The word "kiosk" comes from Turkey and refers to a little open-sided building made of light materials. When we use a kiosk in art activities, it consists of boxes of various sizes, stacked together. They may be stacked in any form you like, but most kiosks are stacked in graduating sizes with a broomstick or large dowel down the center to hold them in place.

Materials needed:
Boxes of various sizes
Broomstick or long dowel
Paper or fabric flag for top
Crayons or markers
Paper to draw on and cover boxes if necessary

Decide which scenes from the story you want to illustrate. Assign the scenes to the students. The scenes are placed on the kiosk in the order in which the story unfolds. The kiosk can also be used to display one scene from several Bible stories. This would be a good way to show the whole church the Bible stories that your class has been studying. Display it at a prominent place in the building.

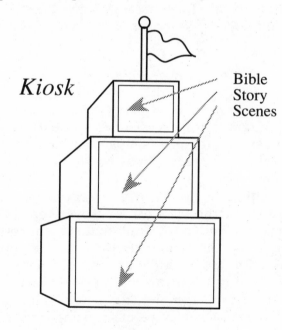

Kiosk — Bible Story Scenes

Mobiles

Mobiles create a three-dimensional effect, and the movement catches your attention. Several students may work together on one mobile, or each student may make a mobile to take home and share with the family. Younger children will need assistance in assembling the mobiles, but most elementary students and youth can accomplish it themselves. Encourage teens to be creative in folding paper, using wires, and so on.

Materials needed:
Hangers for the mobile: coat hangers, paper plates, cardboard paper towel rolls, small tree branch, or dowels
String or yarn for attaching objects to the hanger
Drawings, pictures, or objects made from other media
Scissors, glue, paper, etc.

A mobile is a simple way of telling the story. The hanging objects may be pictures of different characters in the story or drawings of scenes from the story. The mobile is then used as a springboard for storytelling or to illustrate the scenes. If the students take them home, suggest that they use them to tell the story to their family.

Paper Folding

Often we think of paper folding as only appropriate for experienced students. We forget about such simple foldings as a rectangle of paper folded once to form a tent, a long narrow strip folded zig-zag to form a sheepfold, a circle with a slit cut to form a radius and the edges of the cut overlapped to make a yarmulke or skullcap that men wore in Jesus' day and still wear in Hebrew worship. Most middle or older elementary children can learn to fold paper to form a boat. More complicated paper foldings such as doves may be made using origami instructions.

Materials needed:
Medium- to heavy-weight paper. For more complicated foldings, use rice paper, which can be found in art stores.

Stained Glass

Stained glass, as we use it in art activities, is actually a way of treating paper so that it has a stained-glass appearance. This is an appropriate way to experience Bible stories, because that is how our stained-glass windows first came into being. The common people could not read and no printed Bible was available for them, and so the craftsmen began to make pictures from colored glass to use in the church windows. These windows might be called one of our first audio-visual experiences in the church. By looking at the windows, the people could recall the Bible stories themselves.

Materials needed:
White paper (typing weight)
Black construction paper
Pencils, crayons, glue, and scissors
Black permanent marker
Baby oil
Cotton swabs
Table protection and paper towels

For young children, pre-cut the frames from black construction paper. Older children and youth may cut their own. This cut-out space will be where the picture will show through.

Talk about how stained-glass windows were used to tell Bible stories before the printed book. Decide which scene from the Bible story the stained glass will represent.

Place the pre-cut black paper frame over the white paper and trace the outline of the opening. The "opening" area of the picture will later be treated with oil and is what will show through the frame. Inside this open area, draw a picture with pencil and trace over it with black permanent marker. Keep the lines simple. The lines represent the "leaded" part of the window. Use crayons to color all parts inside the opening, including the background.

After protecting the working surface with papers, use cotton swabs dipped in baby oil to coat the back of the paper. Be careful not to use the oil outside the colored area, wiping away any excess with paper towels. Glue the frame around the picture.

(NOTE: For younger children, draw the picture ahead of time. They can do the coloring, but they will need help with the oil and gluing.)

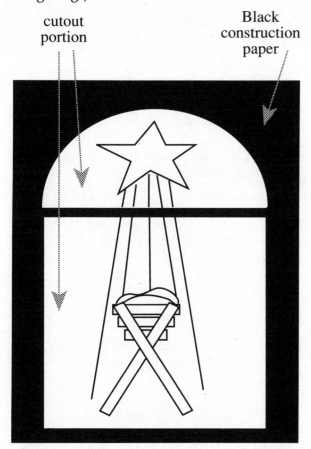

cutout portion

Black construction paper

Story Chain

Most children enjoy making paper chains. Older children can write parts of a Bible story on sections of the chain and use it for telling the story.

Materials needed:
Construction paper of various colors, cut into uniform strips. The strips may be 1 × 6 inches or larger, depending on how much of the story you expect to write on each link.
Glue or tape

Talk about the Bible story and how it is important that we share it with others. With pre-readers, you will want to print sections of the story on the links ahead of time. Early elementary can copy some of it themselves, but the sentences will need to be short and simple. Older children and teens can even decide how to tell the story. After the story has been printed on links, arrange them in the order that the story unfolds. Each link is fastened to the preceding link in order, with the printed side out. The student can then move from link to link, telling the complete story. Younger children can take the chain home and have parents or older siblings read the story to them. Eventually they will tell the story with the chain, even though they cannot read it. Through the story chain they have "met with" the Bible story.

Story Block

Story blocks can be used to tell the story or to review several stories.

Materials needed:
Square box or poster weight paper or cardboard
Crayons or felt-tip markers or Bible pictures
Paper (if desired, to draw on and glue to block sides)

Either use a box or make a cube from poster weight paper or cardboard, using the guide on page 32. If these will be individual story blocks, enlarge the pattern to at least three inches square. If you are making one for the classroom, make it even larger. If you are reviewing several stories, select a scene from each story to be drawn for each side. If you are using the block to tell one story, select six scenes that will remind you of the progress of the story, or select five scenes, using the remaining surface to print the title of the story. After all drawings are completed, place them on the six surfaces of the story block. The story may be told by turning the block.

Story Block

Fold on dotted lines. Fold tabs under and tape, matching tabs with letters.

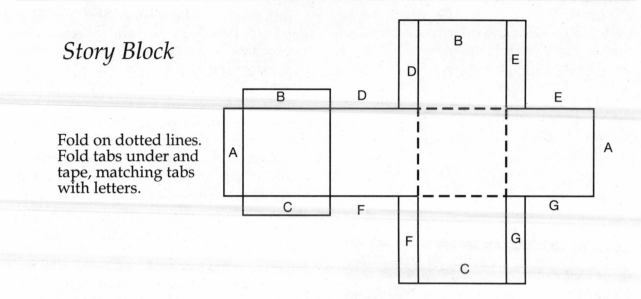

NOTE: A story block may also be made by cutting six teaching pictures in uniform squares and fastening them together along the edges with tape to form a cube or block.

Story Quilt

A story quilt can be as simple or as involved as you like. It is a way to review the story or to illustrate it as you go along.

Materials needed:
A large piece of white fabric marked in squares or several 10- to 12-inch squares of white fabric.
Fabric with a print design to back the quilt and to place between squares, if squares are used.
Crayons, permanent markers, fabric paints, or colored floss and needles
Sewing machine or needle and thread

Decide just which scenes will be illustrated on the quilt. Assign the scenes to the students. They will draw each scene on a square with crayons or fabric paints. If crayons are used, be sure to press the squares with a hot iron and pressing cloth in order to set the colors. If the students are experienced with stitching, they may draw the outline lightly in pencil and embroider it. When washed, the pencil will wash out. These scenes are stitched together and backed,

forming a quilt. After using the quilt in the classroom, display it elsewhere in the church for others to enjoy. Your class may want eventually to give it to someone, passing on the story with the quilt.

NOTE: The quilt may also be made of felt, cutting pieces of colored felt and gluing the scenes in squares on the quilt. The scenes tell the story.

Story Table

A story table is a fun way to tell a progressing story as you go along. It is particularly exciting with stories such as those of Paul and Moses. Each part you study is illustrated on the table until you have covered the complete journeys of Paul or the story of Moses from birth to death.

Materials needed:
A long table or counter (or a sand table from a preschool room)
Brown wrapping paper for the ground, mountains, etc.
Various-size boxes to be covered, for houses, etc.

Mirrors or blue paper for rivers and lakes
Pipe cleaners, clay, fabric, etc., for people
  and animals
Tree branches, etc., for trees
Imagination of ways to create the scenes

As each event in the story is studied, decide
how you will illustrate that event. It is
important that the table remain up from one
session to the next so that it can be built on
and the complete project shared at the end. If
it is portable, it may be moved to a prominent
place in the building and shared with the
whole church family.

TV Show

Television has become so common in our
culture that children and youth easily think in
terms of a story on TV.

Materials needed:
Box about 12 × 15 inches or larger
Shelf paper or another continuous roll of
  paper
Pencils, crayons, markers, etc.
Two dowels
Four spools to attach to dowels to facilitate
  cranking (optional)

Make the television by cutting an opening
in one side of the box for the "screen." The
opening should be a little smaller than the
width of your roll of paper. Cut corresponding holes in the top and bottom of the sides of
the box for the dowels.

Decide which scenes you will use to tell the
story. Divide the roll of paper into sections
the height of the "screen" opening in the box.
Be sure that there is about a foot "lead" of
paper at the beginning and the end of the roll.
Assign scenes in order to the students, and
ask them to draw and color the scenes on the
sections of the long paper. (It may be easier to
have the scenes drawn on typing paper and
glued or taped together.) Attach the end of
the scene series to the lower dowel with tape.
Roll the paper up on this dowel. Next run the
paper up across the "screen" opening and
attach it to the top dowel. You are ready to
begin your TV show, telling the story.

Using Drama to Tell the Story

Drama is one of the most exciting methods of sharing the Bible story. Even Jesus used drama. When he took the basin and the towel and began washing the disciples' feet, he dramatized just how we should care for others. He also used drama when he arranged to enter the city riding on a donkey. It was traditional for the ruler in wartime to ride a horse, but in peace it was traditional to ride a donkey. Jesus dramatized his mission of peace. The breaking of the bread and sharing of the cup during the Passover meal was one of the most dramatic ways Jesus could have used to connect his death with our salvation. And we continue with that drama today as we experience the Lord's Supper or Communion.

Francis of Assisi, through another type of drama, brought the Christmas story to life. He used real animals and carved figures of Mary, Joseph, and the shepherds.

In today's world, all too many children and youth experience drama only as spectators, in front of the television. Drama becomes really vital to children and youth when we *involve* them—in the planning, in the preparation, and in the doing. For drama in education, we do not need an audience. The experience is its own reward. Drama in Christian education is not for perfection, but rather for learning the story by being a part of the story itself.

Often we think that we cannot use drama because we expect it to be a full production of a play. In reality, our children use a form of drama when they play games, such as "housekeeping" and dress-up. Drama has a far broader range than we often recognize. Drama is most effective when it helps students get "into the skin" of the Bible characters, when it helps them catch the feelings that the characters must have had. The more they experience the physical and emotional presence of Bible people and life, the closer they will come to understanding its meaning.

Acting Out

Acting out does not involve memorized script. It is a creative drama, where the students are given the situation and act as they think the characters would act under those circumstances. Use this for "feeling into" or "responding out of" the story. It can be of any length. Younger children need very brief assignments.

It is best to have ample room for movement as you act out a story. Keep the props and costumes simple, if you use any at all. A square of cloth, placed over the head and across the forehead with ends pulled back over the ears, makes a simple headdress. A tunic can be made by cutting a cloth double the length from the shoulder to the knees. Cut a slit and hole for the head in the center, and tie at the waist with a strip of contrasting cloth.

Clowning

Because many churches have elaborate clown ministry programs, we often ignore the possibility of using clowning in the classroom. Clowning can be an exciting way to experience Bible stories. In the classroom it needs to be kept quite simple. It is not even necessary to use face makeup and costumes.

Clowning allows persons to express feelings in ways that they would not ordinarily feel comfortable doing. To ease a group into clowning, ask the whole group to act as a clown would act in these three ways, reminding them that clowns do not talk but express their feelings through their facial expressions and actions:

1) A happy feeling, being playful and bouncy
2) An unhappy feeling, with a sad face and droopy walk, perhaps like a wilting flower
3) Unsure of yourself, falling down and tripping over things, stumbling over feet, clumsy, etc.

These three ways of clowning are the three basic types: white-face, sad-face, and Auguste clown. With older children and youth, you may want to identify the types. With all ages, simply suggest that in clowning we may want to use some of these actions in different stories or for different times in a story. It may be best to use only the first two types of clowning with young children.

All ages might use clowning to "respond out of" the stories of Zacchaeus (Luke 19:1-10) and Jesus' entry into Jerusalem (Mark 11:1-11). Read or tell the story first. Next ask the students how they think each person in the story might feel at specific times. Then either let the students express the feelings of whichever character they choose as you tell the story, or assign persons to clown the characters.

Elementary children and youth will enjoy clowning the feelings in the story of the Good Samaritan (Luke 10:25-37), and youth can use Matthew 25:31-46, where Jesus said, "I was hungry and you fed me."

Charades

The game of charades turns the Bible story review into a fun experience. Older elementary and youth will find this approach particularly exciting. It is best that you use charades in a non-competitive way, simply having the whole class guess the story that is being acted out and not keeping score. Celebrate together each time the story is guessed.

Divide the students into two or more groups. Each group will draw the name of a Bible story from previously prepared slips of paper. If you think it will help, list the names of the characters on the paper. Allow time for the groups to huddle and decide how they will act out the story. Remind them that there is no speaking in charades. It must all be done with movement and gestures.

Creative Movement

Although movement comes natural to children, you will find some children and many youth who are hesitant to express themselves "without a plan." I suggest that you experiment using echo pantomime (see below) with these students before trying creative movement.

Creative movement begins with freeing ourselves to move. Before any experiment with creative movement, spend some time relaxing the body and feeling free to move. Relaxation can be accomplished using some simple games or exercises, such as the following:

1) Act like a boat floating in water or a kite bobbing in the wind.
2) Act like a kitten, asleep on a rug, who begins to wake and stretch.
3) Walk in different ways—jerky, smooth, stiff, floppy, light-footed, or heavy-footed.
4) Sitting on a chair or on the floor, react with the top part of your body as if it were a hammer being used.
5) Act like a flower opening its petals slowly.

Creative movement makes a good "feeling into" activity. Before the story of the Hebrews wandering in the wilderness (Exodus, selected), suggest that the students move as if they had been walking for a long time and were hot and thirsty, or as if they were walking over rough ground.

Creative movement can also be used as a "responding out of" activity by asking the group, after the story has been presented, to express in movement how a particular character might have felt during a specific part of the story.

Echo Pantomime

If your group is new to echo pantomime, explain what an echo is and define pantomime. Explain that you will tell the story in short sentences, with some action, and after each section they will all repeat the sentences and action together.

Echo pantomime is often used in curriculum. I save these on file for future reference. You may also create your own by writing out the story in short sentences. For each sentence (or short group of sentences) plan an action appropriate to the sentence. Practice the story and actions to be sure that they are simple and easy to follow. Sometimes I write the echo pantomime on a large sheet of paper and post it on the wall where I can see it while leading. This example is appropriate for all ages (from Delia Halverson, *Ages 4-6 Invitation, Fall 1983 Teacher Book* [Nashville: Graded Press], p. 45):

Solomon Builds a Temple
(Echo pantomime based on I Kings 5 and 6)

Words	Actions
Long ago people lived in tents.	*Shape tent with hands over head.*
They worshiped God in tents too.	*Step to side, shape another tent.*
God planned for King Solomon to build a temple.	*Make crown for king.*
There were many workers for God.	*Point to many people.*
Some cut the cedar trees;	*Turn right and cut with ax.*
Some cut the cypress trees;	*Turn left and cut with ax.*
Some dug stones from hills;	*Dig with shovel.*
Some hammered the wood;	*Hammer.*
Some put stones together.	*Pile stones together.*
Finally the Temple was finished.	*Spread out arms and smile.*
Everyone sang and shouted with joy!	*Cup hands around mouth.*
And the celebration to God began.	*March in circle, clapping or playing an instrument.*

Mask Drama

Masks give us the illusion of being hidden, and therefore a mask can help us express our feelings or act the part of another without embarrassment.

Masks may be created from simple items such as paper plates (either tied on or held in front of the face with a stick attached to the bottom), paper bags (fringed around the bottom to allow them to come over the shoulders), old pillowcases, or left-over Halloween masks. They can also be elaborately created with paper-mache or commercially produced mixtures. No matter how you make them, the most effective masks show exaggerated emotions that can easily be seen. When creating masks, try them on and cut the eye and mouth openings before decorating the masks.

Try using happy and sad masks to interpret Zacchaeus (Luke 19:1-10) or one of the healing stories (Mark 2:1-12; Mark 7:31-37; Luke 8:40-42, 49-56; Luke 17:11-19; and John 5:1-15). Each student can make a happy mask and a sad mask with paper plates and exchange them at appropriate times during the story.

Puppets

Puppets can either be used in presenting the story, in reviewing the story, or in "feeling into" and "responding out of" the story. Toy stores and television now have such elaborate puppets that we often feel inadequate when we try to make them ourselves. Some churches also have a puppet ministry with a large collection of soft sculpture puppets. These puppets are most often used with pre-taped script versions of the Bible stories. Or a single puppet may be used to tell the story. A unique way of telling the story with a puppet is to pretend that the puppet is shy and let it "whisper" the story, bit by bit, into your ear and you repeat what was "whispered" each time, telling the story for the puppet.

If you are interested in creating soft sculpture or more elaborate puppets, there are several books on the market that will help you. However, don't ignore the real learning potential with simply made puppets, using a sock, a fabric cut with simple head and arms and body, or a paper bag. You might even bring a sewing machine into the classroom and sew up the fabric puppets as they are made. (See illustration on p. 38.)

Another source for puppets is a stuffed toy with the stuffing removed from the body and enough stuffing removed from the head and arms or front legs to allow fingers to be used. Even a puppet made from a stuffed animal can be the narrator, telling the story.

Staging is not necessary. Puppets that tell the story may be used as you sit in a circle. If each student has a puppet and will be working the puppet at the same time, then a circle is the most appropriate room arrangement.

If the story is being "acted" by the puppets and you wish a stage, simply turn a table on its side and have the persons who move the puppets sit on the floor behind the table and hold the puppets above the edge of the table, using the table as the stage. You may also tie a rope across part of the room and drape a blanket over the rope to hide the persons as they manipulate the puppets. Whatever you do, avoid crowding the "back stage" area unless your group has had extensive practice with puppets.

Reporter Interview

Youth and older elementary classes will enjoy planning and staging a reporter interview. Ask the students to view a TV newscast interview before beginning this experience. If you check your television guide and give them a list of possible newscasts, they will be more likely to watch an interview. Ask them ahead of time to think about who was interviewed on the program and the kinds of questions they were asked, whether props such as maps or printed lists were used, and just what type of research the interviewer

Simple fabric puppet

Draw features on front with markers before sewing so that they will not bleed through on back.

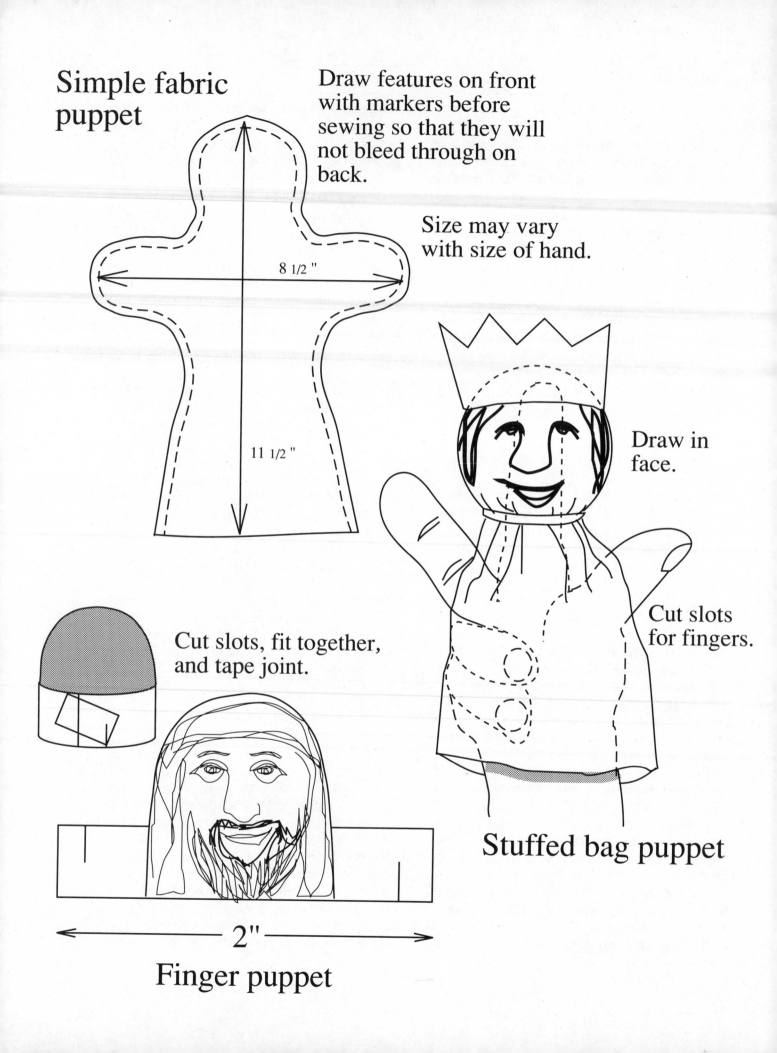

Size may vary with size of hand.

8 1/2 "

11 1/2 "

Draw in face.

Cut slots for fingers.

Cut slots, fit together, and tape joint.

Stuffed bag puppet

← 2" →

Finger puppet

might have needed in order to know what questions to ask.

Collect additional background information for the students to use, such as Bible dictionaries, maps, multimedia resources, encyclopedias, and books on Bible times and customs. Check your church and local libraries for these.

As you begin, talk about the television interviews they watched. Be certain that they know the Bible story you will be using. Review the primary elements of the story and jot these on a chalkboard as a reminder as they work. Introduce the resource material that you have brought in and explain how it is used. Talk about the background information needed in order to know how to conduct a good interview. Assign various students to use the different resources and report back to the group.

After you have researched the background, ask each student to work on two questions that might be asked in the interview. Exchange these questions and have the students write answers. Review the questions and answers in the group. Only factual questions have right and wrong answers. Acknowledge the validity of all answers that deal with how a person might have felt or what he or she might plan to do in the future. With questions of fact, follow the story carefully. Leave speculative answers to the imagination of the students.

Select several questions to use in the interview and set up the interview. If your group is large, you may want to interview several persons who were "at the scene" even if they were not directly involved. This will give opportunity for more persons to be involved (as both interviewers and persons interviewed) and for more questions and answers to be used.

The interview may be videotaped or audiotaped to share with another group or simply in order to see the result.

Photo Drama

We all enjoy seeing ourselves in a picture. To make a photo drama, plan specific scenes that you will use to tell the story. Have the students write the story in their own words. The scenes they describe will then be set up and photographed to illustrate the story. This will be more effective if the characters are in costume, although elaborate backdrops are not necessary. If you do want to make backdrops, consider painting them with tempera paint on opened refrigerator boxes, which easily stand alone. Make a storybook of the Bible story, using the words the class has written along with the photographs. The book may be shared with a younger class.

For a variation of this, make a videotape of the story. This allows more action in telling the story. The parts may be read by persons off camera as the photographs are taped or the videotape may be a narrative that the students as actors follow on camera.

Play Reading

Play readings are ways to use plays without production details and without excessive practice time. The parts are read rather than memorized, but you will want to be sure that the characters have enough reading or drama experience to read the parts well, in a dramatic way. If you wish to "do it up right" have the characters sit on tall stools in front of the audience.

You can use a published play or create your own script, taking the words directly from the scripture. The story of Jesus and the Samaritan woman is an excellent story for a play reading.

Jesus in Samaria
(John 4:1-30 selected GNB)

Narrator: The Pharisees were telling lies about Jesus, and so he left Judea and headed back to Galilee. On his way he passed through Samaria. He was tired when he reached Jacob's well and sat down by the well while his disciples went for food. It was about noon, when most women had already drawn their water and returned home. But a Samaritan woman came to draw water.

Jesus: Give me a drink of water.

Woman: You are a Jew, and I am a Samaritan—so how can you ask me for a drink?

Narrator: Now, Jews in those days did not like Samaritans, and certainly would not use the same cup as a Samaritan.

Jesus: If you only knew what God gives and who it is that is asking you for a drink, you would ask him, and he would give you life-giving water.

Woman: Sir, you don't have a bucket, and the well is deep. Where would you get that life-giving water? It was our ancestor Jacob who gave us this well; and he and his sons and his flocks all drank from it. You don't claim to be greater than Jacob, do you?

Jesus: Whoever drinks this water will get thirsty again, but whoever drinks the water that I will give him will never be thirsty again. The water that I will give him will become in him a spring which will provide him with life-giving water and give him eternal life.

Woman: Sir, give me that water! Then I will never be thirsty again, nor will I have to come here to draw water.

Jesus: Go and call your husband and come back.

Woman: I don't have a husband.

Jesus: You are right when you say you don't have a husband. You have been married to five men, and the man you live with now is not really your husband. You have told me the truth.

Woman: I see you are a prophet, sir. My Samaritan ancestors worshiped God on this mountain, but you Jews say that Jerusalem is the place where we should worship God.

Jesus: Believe me, woman, the time will come when people will not worship the Father either on this mountain or in Jerusalem. You Samaritans do not really know whom you worship; but we Jews know whom we worship, because it is from the Jews that salvation comes. But the time is coming and is already here, when by the power of God's Spirit people will worship the Father as he really is, offering him the true worship that he wants. God is Spirit, and only by the power of his Spirit can people worship him as he really is.

Woman: I know that the Messiah will come, and when he comes, he will tell us everything.

Jesus: I am he, I who am talking with you.

Narrator: Just at that moment, Jesus' disciples returned and were greatly surprised to find him talking with a woman. But none of them said to her, "What do you want?" or asked him, "Why are you talking with her?" Then the woman left her water jar, went back to town, and said to the people there,

Woman: Come and see the man who told me everything I have ever done. Could he be the Messiah?

Narrator: So the people left the town and went to Jesus. Many believed in Jesus because of what the woman said about him, and many believed because of his message.

Other scripture passages that can easily be modified into play readings include:

God Calls Samuel, I Samuel 3:1-10, 19-20
A Woman and Her Son Care for Elijah, I Kings 17:8-15
Jesus Calms the Storm, Mark 4:35-41
Parable of the Forgiving Father, Luke 15:11-32
Friends Traveling to Emmaus, Luke 24:13-35
Jesus Attends a Wedding, John 2:1-12

Role Playing

Role playing enables us to step into the shoes (or role) of persons in a given situation. We most often think of role playing with older elementary and youth, using it to help them think through dilemmas and resolve conflicts.

With young children, modified role playing is frequent in play, such as in make-believe homemaking and dress-up, whether we label it role playing or not. We can easily use such play to help young children "feel into" the story. Using the Bible story of Jesus' boyhood (Luke 2:39-40), bring woodworking tools, wood chips, and wood shavings to a play center. Encourage the children to experiment with the tools under adult supervision. This is a natural entry into explaining that Joseph was a carpenter and Jesus learned about being a carpenter from him. Before the story of Abraham's journey (Genesis 12:1-5), create a play center with a tent and use backpacks and other fabric packs to pretend you are packing for a long journey. If you have a tent that is simple to put up and take down (or using a blanket thrown over a rope), "make" your journey, taking down your tent and carrying it with you. Take your snack on the journey, and stop to eat along the way, remembering that there were no fast food restaurants in those days. This may also be used before telling the story of Mary and Joseph's journey to Bethlehem (Luke 2:1-7), or Jesus' trip to Jerusalem as a boy (Luke 2:41-52).

With older children and youth, the traditional use of role playing is appropriate, using the story up to the point of the dilemma and allowing the participants to finish the story (solve the dilemma) in the way they want. Follow the plan below.

Preparation Ahead of Time:

1. Select the story.

1. Example: Ananias and Saul/Paul—Acts 9:1-19

2. In a sentence or two, describe the dilemma.

2. Saul was known for seeking out and arresting followers of Jesus, and God has told Ananias that he is to go to the house where Saul is and place his hands on him to heal his sight.

3. Decide how much of the story will be read or told before role playing, leaving the solution or decision to be read *after* the role playing.

3. Tell of stoning of Stephen and Saul's approval, and read Acts 8:1-3; 9:1-16.

4. Consider several questions you might ask students after reading the first part of the story but before role playing, to help them relate to the dilemma.

4. How would you feel if you were told to go to help someone who you knew had come to town to arrest you? What were the jail conditions then? What was happening to persons who were arrested for following Jesus?

5. Decide what characters will be in the role playing.

5. Saul, his traveling companions, the host at the house on Straight Street, Ananias, voice of God

6. Think through several endings that the students might come up with.

6. Ananias sending someone else; Ananias telling God that it was too dangerous and he was too important in spreading the gospel to put himself in such a situation; Ananias following God's direction

In the Class Session:

- Review and read the story with the students.
- Select volunteers to play the parts.
- Use the questions you devised in #4 above with both characters and observers.
- Have the characters act out the story, making up their own solution.

- Discuss the solution or solutions and others the class might think of. Other students may act out the new solutions.
- Ask the class to select the solution they prefer and
- Read the solution from the scripture text.

****

Situation Drama

In a situation drama we help the students appreciate the situation in the Bible story. For example, as a "feeling into" activity when studying creation (Genesis 1:1–2:3) with elementary children and youth, introduce chaos into the room (overturned chairs and tables, items about the room, and lights out). Move into the darkened room and ask the students, "What do you suppose it was like before God created light?" After allowing brief discussion, turn on the lights. Then look around the room. Ask them what's wrong with the room. Obviously, it's in chaos or confusion. Tell them that God made order in our world out of chaos or confusion. Suggest that you be co-creators with God, and create order from the confusion of the room. After setting the room in order, you may pray a prayer of thanksgiving for the order that God set in the world.

Other Bible stories that might be used with situation drama include: Jesus Calms the Storm (Mark 4:35-41), acting out being tossed on the waves at sea; Pentecost (Acts 2:1-13) or the tower of Babel (Genesis 11:1-9), giving groups of students the same sentence in different languages to speak to one another.

Tableau or Still Picture

A tableau or still picture can be made using much the same process as the one explained above in the photo drama. For the tableau, set up a framed stage, perhaps using drapes, or cut a frame out of a refrigerator box that has been cut apart to form a screen. Plan your scenes, which will be motionless and silent. A simple way to change scenes is to place a sheet on the floor in front of the scene and have two persons raise the sheet between the scenes, allowing the characters to change places while the sheet is raised. If you have a stage with a curtain, you may use the curtain for the scene changes.

7

Using Writing Activities and Research to Tell the Story

Writing, particularly in Christian education, is undertaken not so much to be read as for gaining an experience of the story. If you grew up in the same sort of school system as mine, then writing was an assignment to see just what you had learned, primarily what you had learned in English grammar. In fact, school writing assignments may have completely squelched all of your writing desires. In using research and writing activities in the church, we need to realize that the learning is in the doing, not in the result.

When I was given my first typewriter as a senior in high school, my father also gave me one of the best gifts I've ever received. He gave me the assignment to type all of my personal letters. And he told me not to worry about how they looked, but simply to "talk with my friends" using the typewriter. That assignment saved me from getting hung up on the mechanics of writing and allowed my feelings to come out on the paper.

One of the best books I've read on children's writing is by Jacqueline Jackson, *Turn Not Pale, Beloved Snail* (Little, Brown & Co., 1974). She suggests that children approach creative writing as a way to record good ideas, what we think and feel inside. You can help your students release their creative writing thoughts if you let them know that their writing, at this point, needs only to be in a form that they can read. If you should decide to print something later for others to read, then you can help the student go back and "edit" it for publication.

Learning happens when the student is personally involved. Writing is creating, and as you can see on the learning ladder below (from Delia Halverson, *How to Train Volunteer Teachers* [Nashville: Abingdon Press, 1991], p. 73) creating is near the top. I have even found that listening to a sermon is more productive when I take notes.

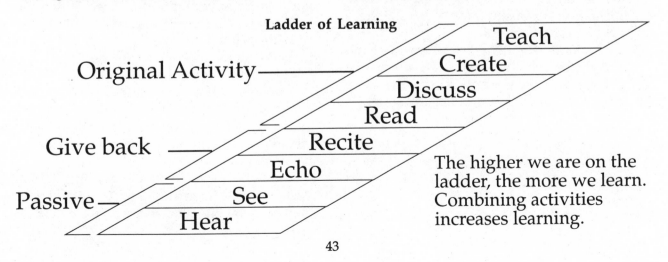

Ladder of Learning

Original Activity — Teach / Create / Discuss / Read

Give back — Recite / Echo

Passive — See / Hear

The higher we are on the ladder, the more we learn. Combining activities increases learning.

Research easily goes hand-in-hand with writing, although research is also beneficial when using Bible stories in other ways. It is important to have research books available for older elementary and youth. Refer to chapter 2 for appropriate ages and specific information on research tools.

Research can help us gain a new perspective on a story or a scripture. Here are some insights I have gained from research on the background of the 23rd Psalm.

Shepherd   Characteristics of shepherds were faithfulness (laying down life for the sheep), tenderness, diligence in searching for a lost sheep, discipline in spending time alone with God, which seemed to give them wisdom.

Leading   Eastern shepherds walk before the flock, and the sheep all know their own shepherd and follow willingly.

Pastures   The shepherd locates good pastures and moves the sheep before they overgraze and spoil the grass.

Still water   Sheep will not drink from rushing water. They will lie down beside a stream of rushing water and die of thirst before they will put their head into it to drink. And so still water is life-giving.

Valley of the Shadow of Death   There is actually such a place, very rough with deep ravines where snakes lurk.

Rod and staff   The rod was used to beat off animals that would kill the sheep, and the staff had a crook and was used to pull sheep to safety or lift them over rocks.

Anointed with oil   Snakes often bit the faces of unsuspecting sheep, and so the shepherd rubbed on healing oil.

"Cup" runneth over   The "cup" was a round trough beside the well into which the shepherd poured water. Without it the sheep could not drink. Again, a life-giving act.

Family Tree

Researching family trees is exciting to some people and nothing but a bore for others. The lineage of Jesus and the line from Abraham to Joseph are the main family trees in the Bible. If you use this activity, spice it up with drawings that depict the main stories along the way. Also add the scripture references. This makes it a good tool for practice in Bible skills.

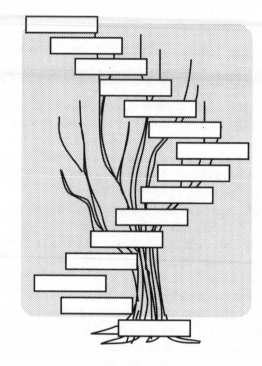

Letters

Letter writing may be a comfortable form of writing for some, but many children and youth have never written a letter. Writing a letter that includes a Bible story can be a form of witnessing. Through the letter, the story may be told to someone who would not hear it in any other way. Ask the students to think of someone whom they might write to tell about the class and what you have been studying. As a part of the letter, have them include a brief version of a Bible story that you have studied.

Another way to use letter writing in the classroom is to have the students pretend that they are someone who observed the action of the story and they are writing a letter to a friend, telling that friend about what happened. Before you begin, have each person describe the pretend "friend" to whom they are writing. This eases them into the experience and makes it less of a writing assignment.

Non-writers may work together as a class on a letter. The class may decide to write it to someone who is ill or a class in a church in another city. Write it on a long sheet of paper and ask them to illustrate the story. Then post it on the wall for a short time before mailing it.

However you use letter writing, it is more exciting if you let the students use real stationery. Perhaps you can find odds and ends of stationery, or parents may be able to provide some miscellaneous stationery. Elementary children will do better with lined paper. You might consider ordinary lined paper and use colorful stickers to decorate the paper and envelope.

Resume Writing

Youth and some older elementary students will be able to work with resume writing. Preparing a resume of a Bible character will require research and give the student a better perspective of the character's achievement.

Another study that might take this form is to look at what God is like and what God does for us by preparing a resume of the shepherd using Psalm 23.

Newspaper Writing

Older elementary and youth can work with a newspaper format to tell the story. Before you begin writing, look at a modern-day newspaper to determine the various parts that might be included. Recognize that there are articles on the weather, traveling conditions, political activity, police activity, local economic conditions, and even a comic strip section. Decide which kinds of articles are appropriate for your newspaper, and assign

various reports to students. A Palm Sunday newspaper, which you might title *Jerusalem Journal*, could include:

- Crowd control, including the number of people camping outside the city and numbers in the Temple each morning.
- A police report of someone who was injured as the crowd pushed through the gate to follow Jesus.
- Food costs that were up because of increased demand during the influx of people for Passover.
- Road conditions on the incoming highways and those roads being repaired.
- A society section on persons visiting dignitaries.

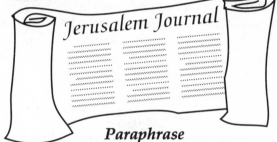

Paraphrase

Paraphrasing is one of the best ways to understand and get to the real content of a Bible story. To paraphrase is to put the story into words other than those of the author, but to retain the real meaning of the story. Actually, when you "tell" the Bible story in your own words you are using a form of paraphrase.

Older children and youth can take a story, read it, and work on paraphrasing. It is often helpful for them to do a little background research about the time and location of the story or about the specific activity involved in the story before they paraphrase it. The section in chapter 2 on Bible translations and reference tools (page 18) will help here.

With young children, read or tell the story first and give them a little background information, such as "there were no motels along the road then, and so they often carried tents on a journey." Ask the young children to tell the story in their own words while you write it down. You may want to use a tape recorder to assist you.

Word Portraits

Talk with your students about just what a portrait is. Discuss how it is different from a photograph. A photograph tells it just as it looks, but a portrait will often bring out the personality of the person or let you see the "real person." Portraits can also center in on the person or object, blocking out the surrounding scenery.

Word portraits use words to express the real feeling and even experience of a person. For instance, instead of simply saying, "One leper returned to thank Jesus," a word portrait might include a description of how the leper kept looking at his arms with disbelief, or how, when he came back, he turned from one person to another, even in between his words to Jesus, asking the persons to look at his healed arms (Luke 17:11-19).

Poetry

There are very few of us who will ever be published poets, but inside all of us is a hidden poet. Recognize that some styles of poetry will appeal to some students and other styles to other students. Help them realize that poetry does not have to rhyme. Try different styles at different times. After you have used a variety of styles, students will recognize which ones they can use to best express their feelings. Then you may allow them to choose their own style. Be aware, however, of new students who may not have had opportunity to experiment with all the styles. Never just say, "Write a poem about the story." We all need more guidance than that.

Several examples of poetry styles follow. Children with handwriting skills can work on the poetry more independently. With young children, talk about it as a group and decide what you will say in the poem, and then write a group poem. Use the poem frequently in the class, so that the younger child remembers what you wrote and can appreciate it.

1. *Picture poems* use words or phrases to outline the shape of an object. The story will need to be told very briefly for this kind of poem. It is best if the picture or shape symbolizes the story. For your first experiences with this form of poetry, suggest the shape and plan the words together as a class. When the students are familiar with the method, they may select their own shapes or symbols.

Jonah and the Fish

Jonah did not want to do as God asked him to. He ran away to sea. But God used a storm to make him listen and obey.

2. Cinquain (sin-cane) poetry may sound complicated, but it is actually one of the simplest forms for creative thinking. It gives structure to the creating, yet the writer retains free expression within the structure. You may want to have a thesaurus handy when using cinquain poetry, but do not become reliant on it. The cinquain poem has five lines, following this formula:

Line 1: One-word title or subject
Line 2: Two words that tell about the story. These words may compose a phrase, or they may be separate words.
Line 3: Three verbs or action words (such as "ing" words) or a three-word phrase about the story
Line 4: Four words that tell of feelings in the story
Line 5: The subject word again, or another word that refers back to the title or subject.

* * * *

Zacchaeus
Unloved   short
Climbed the tree
Was loved by Jesus
Repentant
(Luke 19:1-10)

* * * *

Moses
Hebrew   Egyptian
Led God's people
Worried exasperated trusting confident
Leader
(Exodus, selected)

* * * *

3. Free verse comes in various forms. It may include phrases, sentences, or a series of words, and the lines may vary in length. Action words move the story along in this verse form.

To the wilderness He went,
   wandering for forty days.
"Soooo, you are hungry!
   Turn the stones into bread!"
   . . . but He would not.
"Soooo, look at the kingdoms of the world!
   Worship me and it is yours!"
   . . . but He would not.
"Soooo, throw yourself down from these heights,
   And, you will be saved in a spectacle!"
   . . . but He would not.
And Jesus went forth to accomplish His ministry.
(Luke 4:1-15)

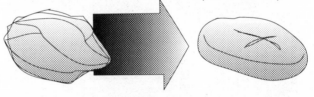

Time Line

A time line will involve some writing and a lot of research. Time lines have no meaning for children who do not have a grasp of history. If you are in doubt about your age group, check with school teachers or look at their school textbooks. If they are using time lines in school, then you know that the students' understanding is mature enough to grasp the concept. As you work with setting up the time line and deciding just what you will use, check the resource section of your Bible. This will give you a guide, but you do not want to simply give the students a time line to copy. Rather, give them Bible references to look up and research references to use to find the approximate times to place on the line. Remember that the research is important for the students, but you must do your own research first in order to guide them. (See illustration on p. 48.)

Major and Minor Prophets

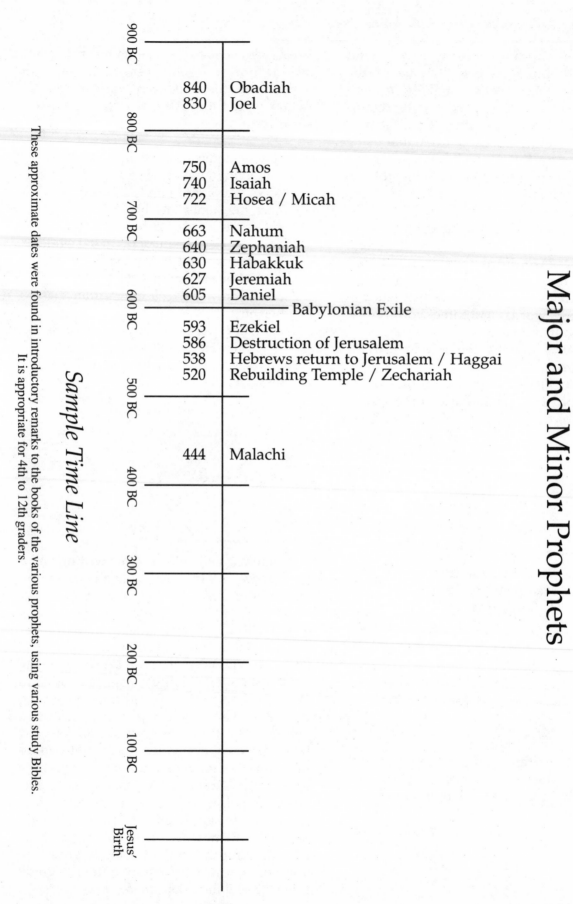

900 BC		
	840	Obadiah
	830	Joel
800 BC		
	750	Amos
	740	Isaiah
	722	Hosea / Micah
700 BC		
	663	Nahum
	640	Zephaniah
	630	Habakkuk
	627	Jeremiah
	605	Daniel
600 BC		Babylonian Exile
	593	Ezekiel
	586	Destruction of Jerusalem
	538	Hebrews return to Jerusalem / Haggai
	520	Rebuilding Temple / Zechariah
500 BC		
	444	Malachi
400 BC		
300 BC		
200 BC		
100 BC		
Jesus' Birth		

Sample Time Line

These approximate dates were found in introductory remarks to the books of the various prophets, using various study Bibles. It is appropriate for 4th to 12th graders.

C H A P T E R
8

Using Games to Tell the Story

Playing games is fun, and so we are surprised when we hear that games can be real learning experiences. Since games can be used as tools for learning, I suggest that every teacher have a handy tool chest of games to draw on.

You may purchase elaborate Bible review games at Christian bookstores. Many of them are good; some are rather lengthy and complicated, even for adults; and most of them are really out of reason in price. They seem particularly high-priced when we consider that most churches have already purchased a wide assortment of games when they purchase curriculum. We need to make a habit of recycling this curriculum instead of throwing out the games.

One of my favorite pastimes is going through old curriculum and salvaging games. Teachers' books will often have games for large groups, and student books, and classroom kits have games for individuals and small groups.

Some of the games require small boxes for storage, but most of them I mount on the inside of manila file folders, labeling them by subject and age appropriateness and filing them for future use. If the game is apt to be used a lot, then I take it to the local school supply store where they will laminate it for a small cost per foot. You can also purchase a laminating plastic at office supply stores. If there are markers, playing cards, or game pieces, I place these inside a marked envelope and place it in the file folder. Periodically through the year, our education committee holds curriculum parties where we go through stacks of old student and teacher books, scissors in hand.

As you use curriculum, keep the games that students enjoy. Use them later for "fill-in" times or when two or three students have finished their work earlier than other students. Have them available as students arrive, particularly for early comers.

Selecting and Creating Games

As you select and create games, your first consideration is the purpose of your game. Write that purpose out in a brief sentence. Although you may have a purpose in mind, writing it on paper will make it firm. There are times when you will play a game to give students practice in telling a Bible story. Other times you may play the game only to familiarize them with names and places. Or you may play the game in order to give them an experience similar to that felt by a character in the story, and no biblical reference at all will be used during the game. As a "feeling into" activity, you can discuss how they felt about the game experience and then follow it up with the story.

Keep your purpose in mind, while considering these points:

1) Is the reading level appropriate?
2) Will the game accommodate the number in your group or can you divide into smaller groups?
3) Can persons who are onlookers also learn?
4) When can an onlooker join in the action?
5) Is there an element of chance?
6) Is the game more cooperative than competitive?
7) Does the game allow decisions?
8) How long will it take? (Think about attention-span expectations.)
9) What discussion or statements are necessary prior to the game?
10) What sort of group response can you have following the game?

Adapting Games

Be aware of ways that you can adapt nonbiblical games. An adaptation of the Alphabet Game is to say, I am going to _____ (naming a biblical city) and I am going to take A _____ (naming something or some person from the Bible that starts with "A," such as Antioch's greetings). The next person repeats, adding something starting with "B," and on through the alphabet.

In an adaptation of the Animal Game, divide the Bible story into scenes. If there are four scenes, select a word or short phrase that tells about one of the scenes. Each person will be given one of these words or phrases. On a given signal, everyone walks around the room blindfolded or with eyes closed, saying out loud the name of the scene and trying to find other persons saying the same word. When all who have the same word are together, have them either draw a picture or plan actions to depict the scene. By presenting the pictures or actions in sequence, the story is told.

You will find two other adaptations under Active Games, below.

Active Games

Children and youth both need active games, particularly when the sessions become lengthy. Plan your games so that they fit the Bible theme. Young children will enjoy Statue, where they move about to music and when the music stops they must freeze in a certain position. You might ask them to freeze as one of the animals on Noah's ark (Genesis 6:14, 19-22; 7:17; 8:1-20; 9:13-15). You can also review parts of a Bible story with the game Simon Says by calling out things like "Simon says step carefully so as not to step on the frogs that God sent to Pharaoh's court" (Exodus, selected) or "Simon says to pull the large net of fish into Peter's boat" (John 21:1-14).

Older children and youth will enjoy the following biblical adaptations:

Mob Chase (adaptation of Red Rover). This game should be played in a large room or outdoors.

Divide the class into three groups. One group will be the Thessalonians, another group the Bereans, and the third group, Paul and his companions.

The Thessalonians and Bereans will stand in lines across from each other, fifty feet apart. Both groups will have their backs to the center. Paul and his companions will come from Philippi (a given point) and walk to the Thessalonians. They will shake hands with them (whose backs are still turned).

At this point, number off the Thessalonians. The even numbers will respond to Paul's teachings positively, the odd numbers will reject Paul's teachings. Then Paul and his companions leave Thessalonica and go toward the Bereans.

After they have left, but before they reach the Bereans, the Thessalonian with the number 1 calls out "mob" and all those who have odd numbers turn and run after Paul and his companions. The even-numbered

Thessalonians cheer Paul and his companions on to the Bereans.

When the Bereans hear Paul and his companions coming, they call to them to come inside. Then the Bereans form a circle around Paul and his companions by holding hands. A few of Paul's companions will likely be caught before reaching the Bereans.

Play the game at least three times, allowing each group an opportunity to play each of the three positions (Acts 17:1-15). (From Delia Halverson, *Grades 5-6 Teacher, Vacation Bible School* [Nashville: Graded Press, 1987], p. 45.)

Shipwreck (adaptation of fruit basket turnover). All players except one sit in a circle with no vacant places. Each player is given the name of a place Paul visited. The player designated captain begins walking around the outside of the circle slowly, telling a story about Paul's adventure and using names of the places in the story. (Don't worry about accuracy. The purpose of the game is fun and to make the names more familiar.)

As each player's place is called, the player rises to follow the captain. When the captain calls out "shipwreck," then all persons find a seat, and the person without a seat becomes the captain for the next round. If the captain calls out "full cargo," then everyone stands and follows the captain until he or she calls "shipwreck." The person left without a place becomes the next captain. Be certain each "retired" captain has a place name (Acts 13–28). (From Delia Halverson, *Grades 5-6 Teacher, Vacation Bible School* [Nashville: Graded Press, 1987], p. 47.)

Scavenger Hunts

Scavenger hunts are excellent ways to sharpen Bible research skills. If students are not at the same skill level, divide the class into groups, with each group having persons with advanced skill levels. Each person may work independently on certain questions, but answers are shared with the whole team.

In the scavenger hunt, the players are given lists of items to find. Concordances, cross reference Bibles, and Bible dictionaries may be used to find the items (answers). If you work in teams, each team should have the same resource books.

The items or questions can be specifically about your current study subject, or they may cover other areas. You might consider some of these:

- Give the professions of the following Bible characters.
- List a book in each of the following sections of the Bible.
- Name three cities that were located near the Sea of Galilee.
- Give two Bible references for the listing of the Ten Commandments.
- What Gospels give the Beatitudes?
- What verses in the Psalms are used in the Beatitudes?

Card Games

One of the advantages to card games is that they are easily made. The only materials needed are cards and felt markers. Blank playing cards are available in many school supply stores, or they can be ordered from Brethren House Ministries (6301 56th Ave. N. St. Petersburg, FL 33709). Even 3 × 5 file cards can be used, although they do not shuffle very easily.

There are several card games that can be adapted to help students learn Bible stories or become familiar with biblical characters. Rummy, Go Fish, and Old Maid are favorites that many children and youth already know. Adapt them by making "books" of Old Testament stories, New Testament stories, parables, wisdom books, cities Paul visited, disciples, major and minor prophets, and so on.

Concentration is a game that all ages can play. Even young children can enjoy it if you use symbols or pictures instead of words. For the game, pairs of cards are made (two identical for each item, person, place, etc.).

You can also use pictures from old curriculum student leaflets. Older children and youth can play with paired cards that have related symbols or words or that have the question on one card of the set and the answer on the other.

To play Concentration, all cards are shuffled and then laid out face down in rows, forming a rectangle. Taking turns, players turn over two cards. If the cards match, they are set aside and that player continues to turn over cards until coming up with unmatched cards. When the cards do not match, they are returned to their original position (face down) and everyone tries to remember where specific cards are in order to match cards later in the game. When all cards have been turned over, the player with the most pairs is the winner. A less competitive way to play the game is to set a timer, letting everyone take turns turning over one pair of cards. The object is for the whole group to see how many pairs they can match in the allotted time. You may also use a stop watch to clock the length of time it takes the whole class to pair up all the cards. In this version, the whole class works to better their total time.

Cards may also be used for sequence games. The object of these games is to put the cards in some sort of order. The cards may be made with sequences of a Bible story, time-line sequences, books of the Bible, and so forth. For this game, each player has a separate set of cards. The cards are shuffled and then each player proceeds to place them in order. Rather than have them play against one another, encourage students to work to improve their own time record. In our fifth-grade class one year, we made a set of cards for each student using the names of the books of the Bible. We used different-colored cards for each group of books, such as Old Testament history, wisdom, major and minor prophets, gospels, and so on. They used the cards in class, and at the end of the year they took them home.

Board Games

Since board games can be played over and over, your work in creating them really pays off. Once students know how to play the game, simply having it out on a table invites them to play.

I have devised a basic gameboard which I use for games with various subjects. In the spaces that tell the player to go ahead, I write a positive aspect of the story (such as "You helped Zacchaeus climb the tree"). In spaces that tell the player to go back, I write negative actions (such as "You pushed someone down trying to get to the front of the crowd to see Jesus"). You will find this basic gameboard on the page opposite. You may reproduce it for your classroom use. The students can take part in creating the game if you talk about the story and allow them to decide what should go into each marked square. If you mount the game on a larger board or paper, they can illustrate it with drawings or pictures from old curriculum. Your class may enjoy making an extra-large gameboard by drawing the game with marking pens on a white plastic tablecloth or a white window shade.

_____
(Title)

Directions:

1. Select a marker for each player.

2. Cut 5 small squares of paper the same size, numbering them 1–5. Mix them up and place in a box.

3. Draw a number. Highest number plays first. (If more than 5 play, each draws a number and puts it back.)

4. In turn, draw a number and move marker that number of spaces. Return number to box.

5. Draw and play until all players complete game.

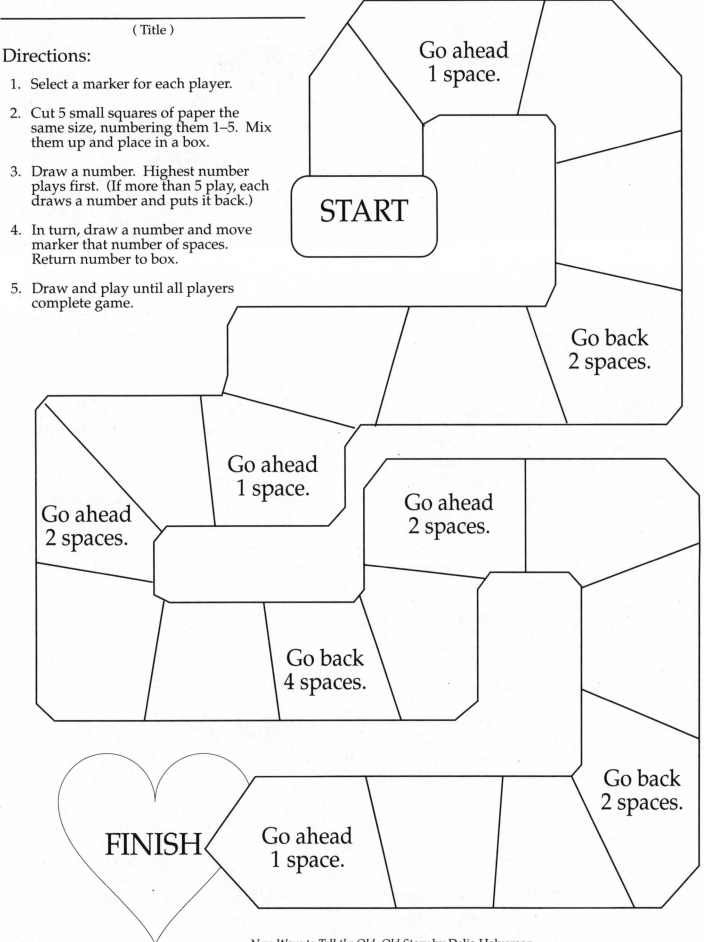

Go ahead 1 space.

START

Go back 2 spaces.

Go ahead 1 space.

Go ahead 2 spaces.

Go ahead 2 spaces.

Go back 4 spaces.

Go back 2 spaces.

FINISH

Go ahead 1 space.

Using Puzzles and Paper to Tell the Story

Because puzzle and paper activities are in most curriculum materials, we sometimes overuse them. Do not rely solely on this sort of Bible story reinforcement, but sprinkle it among other activities. Although we usually plan puzzles and paper activities for elementary and youth, don't forget that preschoolers can participate in these when we draw symbols or use cut-out pictures from old curriculum.

Word searches or crossword puzzles help students become familiar with biblical words. You will find many of these in old curriculum materials, or you may want to create your own. By laminating the puzzles and using grease pencils, they may be used over and over.

Code Puzzles

Code puzzles may be used to familiarize students with places, persons, and words in the Bible. You may also use a code for the letters in sentences that tell a specific story or to give answers to questions about a story. Most code puzzles are for readers, but young children will enjoy the rebus story, which is a kind of code puzzle. In it the story is written, which can be read to the child, but when a particular word is needed, a picture that refers to the word appears instead of the word. The child looks at the picture and supplies the word.

To create a code puzzle, devise your own code to the alphabet. You may exchange letters, or you may insert special symbols for particular letters, such as a heart for each "B," a flower for "S," a star for "M," and so forth. Print up the code so that the students have it available as they work on the puzzle. Example:

♡=B ✿=S ☆=M ⊕=T □=G ◎=R

□od ✿poke ⊕o ☆o✿e✿

⊕h◎ou□h a ♡u◎nin□

♡u✿h.

An interesting way to approach a code puzzle with students who have studied the persecution of the early Christians, is to pretend that you are living during the time of persecution and must send a message that you don't want the authorities to understand (the book of Revelation was written under such conditions and uses codes).

Bouncing Ball Puzzles

Bouncing ball puzzles have several circles, connected by dotted lines, indicating that the ball is bouncing from one place to another. A sentence may be written inside each circle or ball, and the sentences will tell the Bible story. Or there may be drawings of scenes inside each circle. By using the pictures as clues, the student can tell the story by following the bouncing ball from circle to circle. A variation of this is "Follow the Sheep." Use drawings of sheep, running across the countryside. Within each sheep will be a clue to the next part of the story.

Follow the Sheep

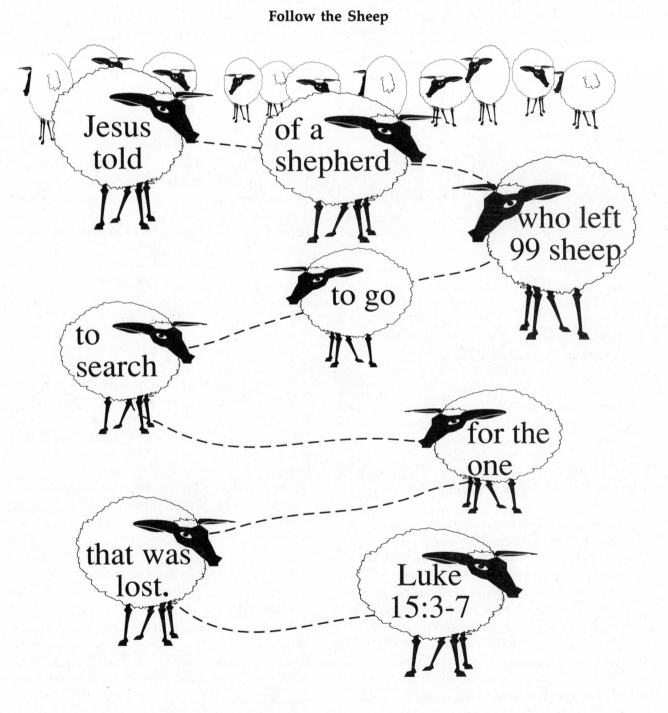

Character Profile

As you study biblical characters, make a large "gingerbread man" outline of a person. This may be done freehand, or you may ask a student to lie on a large piece of paper while you draw around him or her. Hang this on the wall, and as you study the Bible person, write on the paper characteristics of the person that you discover throughout your study.

Continuum

Continuums are used in order to give students opportunity to respond to a story with their own feelings. Continuums usually include a line, where students may place a mark closer to one end or the other, depending on the degree to which they agree or disagree with the statement. Sometimes numbers from 1 to 10 are used on the line, with 10 indicating the greatest agreement.

Continuums are best used with statements that require the student to make a choice.

Jesus' parable of the workers in the vineyard (Matthew 20:1-16) is a good story for a continuum. Some of the statements you might use with this are:

- The owner of the vineyard should have told the first workers that he would hire others later in the day.
agree _____ disagree
- The owner of the vineyard should have paid the first workers more after he hired the others.
agree _____ disagree
- The owner of the vineyard should have paid the later workers less because they didn't work as long.
agree _____ disagree
- The later workers will be eager to work for the vineyard owner in the future.
agree _____ disagree

Follow-up discussion after working with the continuum: Christ taught that God gives us love and salvation, even without works. However, we respond to God's love through our service.

Crossword Puzzles

I cannot say truthfully that everyone loves crossword puzzles, because as a child I hated them. In fact, I still do not enjoy working them, but I do like to create them. Perhaps my poor spelling has something to do with that. Words intrigue me, but my spelling is a joke in our family. When you use crossword puzzles, remember that we are not teaching spelling but are using the puzzle as a tool for learning Bible stories.

Crossword puzzles are easier to make than you would expect. Begin by making a grid or use large graph paper. The questions that you will use must have one-word answers. Write several possible questions and answers before placing any words on the grid. Look at the words and select one that has several letters in it that are beginning letters in other answer words. Place that word in the center of the grid and begin to fill in with the other words, building on the first word, and then on other words. Work with a pencil, because you will need to erase and rearrange words from time to time. A Bible dictionary will help you select questions and words. When the words are in place, number them according to whether they go down or across and re-arrange your questions to correspond. This becomes your answer puzzle, and now you will need to make the blank one for the students to use. To do this, transfer only the numbers on the grid and the questions in their order. For younger children, you may want to place an occasional letter on the grid to help them along.

Jigsaw Puzzle

Jigsaw puzzles are great for individual work. They may be used for early arrivals or for students who finish an assignment before others. Students can often work in pairs with a puzzle.

I have also used large teaching picture puzzles (see directions for making, below) as a closing worship experience with older elementary and youth. Standing in a circle as a group, each student should be given a piece of the puzzle and asked to reflect on the story. Then give the students time to put the puzzle together on the floor in the middle of the circle. Close with a prayer, thanking God for the event (parable, etc.) that the picture puzzle represents and telling God that you will all support one another in whatever message the story has brought you.

Most churches purchase several identical teaching packets, to be used in different classrooms during the quarter. If your curriculum materials are saved and pictures are stored in a central file, you will find that you have multiples of the same teaching picture. Select extra teaching pictures of favorite Bible stories and mount them with rubber cement on light poster board. You may recycle old poster board for this. When it is dry, cut the picture into puzzle pieces and package them in plastic bags or small boxes. Label the container with the name of the story and the appropriate age. File according to the subject of the puzzle.

Map Making

The inability of young children to group abstract concepts does not allow them to transfer locations to a map. Middle elementary children can deal with simple maps, and older elementary and youth should be able to work with them easily. On page 58 you will find a basic map that you may use with students. Consult your Bible atlas or the maps in your Bible to locate cities for specific activities. Here are a few activities you may want to consider:

- Plot Abram's journey from Ur to Egypt.
- Follow Moses' life.
- Locate Naomi's homes.
- Plot David's battles before and after he became king.
- Plot Mary and Joseph's journey from Nazareth to Bethlehem, to Egypt, and back to Nazareth.
- Locate the communities where Jesus taught and healed.
- Follow the footsteps of Jesus in his last week.
- Plot the journeys of Paul, using black for his trip prior to his conversion and different colors for each missionary journey.
- Locate the cities to whom the Revelation of John was written.

Matching Pairs

Matching pairs use pictures or questions and answers in two rows. The object is to draw lines between those that match, those that are related (such as the manger and baby Jesus, camel and crown, sheep and shepherd), or those that answer the question.

For nonreaders, either draw pictures or cut out matching (related) pictures from old curriculum.

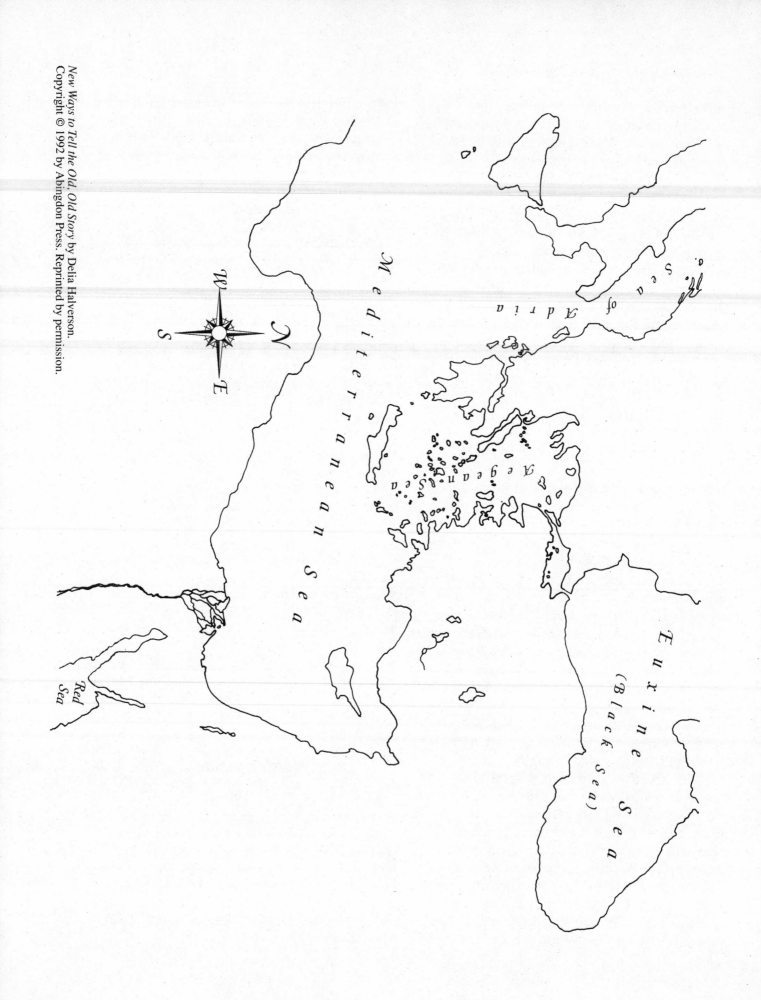

Maze

The maze is an ideal puzzle activity for a study of a time event, such as Holy Week or Joseph's life, or a Bible story that follows a journey. Save mazes from old curriculum. By placing a sheet of plastic over them or laminating them, they can be used again and again with a grease pencil.

The sample below can be adapted to any study by adding pictures cut from old curriculum to illustrate it. You can also move some lines in order to give the maze variety if you want to use it again with the same students.

New Ways to Tell the Old, Old Story by Delia Halverson.

Tic Tac Toe

Most of us learned Tic Tac Toe at an early age. A Bible version can be made easily, using a grid of nine squares, three to a side. In each square draw a symbol or picture to illustrate a particular Bible story or verse. For readers, you can write questions in the squares. Each player selects one square and tells the story, recites the verse, or answers the question. Then he or she places a marker on it. The object is to place three markers in a row in any direction, up or down or diagonally.

A fun way to play this as a group is to make the grid on a large square of fabric or plastic. Then work in teams. Taking turns, a person from each team tells the story or recites the verse and stands in the square, instead of using a marker. When the player stands in the square he or she puts on a sash with the team's color, so that you can see when a team has three in a row.

Word Search

Readers can enjoy a word search. Letters are placed on the page in rows. At places in the page of letters, certain words are placed. The object is to circle the words as you find them among the letters. The words may be printed horizontally, vertically, or diagonally. The list of words to be found is usually placed at the bottom of the page, upside down. In the example below, the answers are not listed, because they are words found in the Lord's Prayer.

Jesus Teaches About Prayer
(Luke 11:1-4; Matthew 6:7-15)

```
J I Y R L H O F A T H E R I L H F E Q U M K I N G D O M K
O K Y I M G E G P H O K G D A M B C Z I O N V E O O L M G
K U H F S R W T U Y P P K L G J M T D E O N H H K N O N F
K B E B Y E X R Y J K X U J B D B K D A V H E A V E N M U
L O B T E M P T A T I O N K K U N R O M F K P L K N C K F
K Y B M N E A O L F J U T K B X C J E K N L N L P M B D G
F O R G I V E I B K L P T E M U O N A A I R I O M O B D G
K H D O L N A O P H G K J Y E V Z L O M D I M W L H F T S
L H Y V F D R L K P M B M F U I N H T R W E R E T Y U I O
A S D F G J T H J K L Z X C V B N M Q W E R T D Y U I P A
S X C V B Y H C B W U R X K R D G E S B E G C F H E Y S C
```

There are ten words from the Lord's Prayer hidden here.

10

Using Music, Rhythm, and Readings to Tell the Story

Sing for joy to God our strength;
  shout aloud to the God of Jacob!
Begin the music, strike the tambourine,
  play the melodious harp and lyre.
                  Psalm 81:1-2 (NIV)

I find it hard to imagine a campfire without singing or rhythm of some sort. Since our Bible stories were first passed from generation to generation around campfires, it is likely that there was song along with the stories. In fact, many of the stories were probably told in a chant.

We use music, rhythm, and readings in Christian education as tools. Although, we may perform using these tools, we must remember that our aim is not performance but practicality. The primary purpose is to help our students learn the stories and apply them to their lives. When they have opportunity to share the story with others, they are learning to witness.

Many of us feel that singing and leading singing is not our particular gift. We do well to remember that we are not expected to "perform" either. We are leading the students in a learning experience. There are

many sing-along tapes today that will help you, or you can ask a musician in your church to play and sing the songs on an audiotape that you can use in the classroom. Multiple copies of the tape also can be made for the students to take home and practice. Rhythms and readings also give variety to the Bible stories.

Hymnals and Songbooks

There are many songbooks on the market. My favorites are *Psalms and Songs* for preschool and elementary ages, *Rejoice and Sing Praise* for elementary ages, and *Sing and Be Joyful* for young children (see page 76). These books have a variety of songs that tell Bible stories and use scripture. Older elementary and youth will particularly enjoy using songs from films and various musicals they may be learning in choir.

Check your hymnal for hymns that are taken from the Psalms or that tell Bible stories. Most hymnals have an index of scripture. There are many hymns that use psalms. Here are a few you may consider that use Bible stories.

O God Who Shapes Creation	Genesis 1:1–2:3
We Are Climbing Jacob's Ladder	Genesis 28:10-17
Go Down, Moses	Exodus 3:7-12
To a Maid Engaged to Joseph	Luke 1:26-38
Silent Night, Holy Night	Luke 2:6-20
It Came Upon the Midnight Clear	Luke 2:8-14
While Shepherds Watched Their Flocks by Night	Luke 2:8-14
We Three Kings of Orient Are	Matthew 2:1-12
Canticle of Simeon	Luke 2:29-32
Jesus Calls Us o'er the Tumult	Matthew 4:18-22
Tell Me the Stories of Jesus	Matthew 19:13-15; Luke 18:15-17
Hosanna, Loud Hosanna	Mark 11:1-11
Up from the Grave He Arose	Matthew 27:57–28:8; Luke 24:1-12; John 20:1-18
On the Day of Resurrection (Emmaus)	Luke 24:13-35
Spirit of the Living God	Acts 1:4–2:47

Creating Songs

We learn best when we create. This is true with songs as well as art activities. Children and youth will also appreciate their songs more when they create them. You can use verses direct from the Bible or paraphrase the story, using simple sentences. Then follow these steps as you work with the students in creating the music (from Delia Halverson, *How to Train Volunteer Teachers* [Nashville: Abingdon Press, 1991], Handout 19).

1. Take one phrase at a time. Read or say it together for the "pulse" or rhythm.
2. Several students speak the phrase with the same rhythm. Listen to how some speak high, and some speak low. Refer to this as "color" sounds. Affirm uniqueness.
3. Listen again to the rise and fall and ask if any student will try to duplicate it with music. You may need to give a tone. Use the key of C and play C, E, G.
4. Sing the phrase several times using the student's tune.
5. Move to other phrases, periodically repeating the whole song.

You may also use familiar tunes to put Bible stories to music. Simple songs for this are "Are You Sleeping, Brother John," "The Farmer in the Dell," and "Twinkle, Twinkle, Little Star."

Try singing the names of the disciples to "Oats, Peas, Beans, and Barley Grow."

Pe-ter, John, and two named James,
An-drew, Mat-thew, Phi-lip too.
Tho-mas, Si-mon, Bar-thol-o-mew,
And Ju-das one and Ju-das two.

Or try these words to "Row, Row, Row Your Boat."

Ma-ry had a child. We call him Je-sus Christ.
Shep-herds came; wise men came.
To praise and wor-ship him.

Rhythm

Rhythm can be used without music to tell a Bible story or to learn Bible verses. Write the story in a few short sentences. Then read the story out loud, listening to the rhythm of the words. Do the words flow in a smooth pace, or is there punctuated excitement? Does part of the story have more emphasis than another? If there are special phrases that you can repeat, use the same rhythm each time they are repeated. As you work with it, you may need to change some wording. Once you think you have the words right, try clapping out the rhythm as you tell the story.

Look at the example on the next page.

Example, using Genesis 1:1 – 2:3 (clap for each x) :

In the be – gin – ning; in the be – gin – ning,

♩ ♩ ♪ ♩   ♪ ♪ ♩ ♪ ♩ ♪
x   x   x   x   x   x   x   x   x   x

God cre – at – ed the heavens and earth.

♩ ♪ ♪ ♪   ♪ ♩ ♩ ♩
x   x   x   x   x   x   x

From the dark, God made light

♩ ♪ ♩ ♩   ♩ ♩
x   x   x   x   x

And it was good!

♪ ♩ ♩ ♩
x   x   x   x

God then made the heav'n a – bove,

♩ ♪ ♩ ♪   ♩ ♪ ♩
x   x   x   x   x

And it was good!

♪ ♩ ♩ ♩
x   x   x   x

God made the earth and trees and flowers,

♪ ♩ ♪ ♩   ♪ ♩ ♪ ♩
x   x   x   x

And it was good!

♪ ♩ ♩ ♩
x   x   x   x

The sun and moon and stars ap - peared,

♪ ♩ ♪ ♩   ♪ ♩ ♪ ♩
x   x   x   x

And it was good!

♪ ♩ ♩ ♩
x   x   x   x

Fish swam the sea; birds flew the air,

♪   ♩   ♪   ♩   ♪   ♩   ♪   ♩
    x   x   x   x

And it was good!

♪   ♩   ♩   ♩
x   x   x   x

And a – ni – mals walked up – on the land,

♩ ♪ ♪ ♪   ♩ ♪   ♩ ♪ ♪
   x x x   x   x x x

And it was good!

♪   ♩   ♩   ♩
x   x   x   x

And then God thought,

♪   ♪   ♩   ♩
    x   x   x

"I'll make boys and girls, and grown – ups too,"

♪ ♪ ♪ ♪ ♪ ♪ ♪   ♪ ♩
   x   x   x x   x

And it was good!

♪   ♩   ♩   ♩
x   x   x   x

And then God rest – ed, pleased with the world.

♪ ♩ ♩ ♪ ♪ ♩ ♩ ♪ ♩
  x x x   x x x x

A – men! A – men!

♪   ♩   ♪   ♩
x   x   x   x

Rhythm may also be used to show emotion in a Bible story. Clapping your knees with your hands at various speeds can enhance the story of Moses and the Hebrews as they escaped Pharaoh. Clapping your knees slowly helps to give a feel for dragging feet as the Israelites wandered in the wilderness (Exodus, selected). Pounding your knees in marching fashion indicates the march around the walls of Jericho, and rapid clapping can indicate the tumbling walls (Joshua 6:1-20).

Choral Reading

You may devise a choral reading from a psalm or from a story. The reading is usually done antiphonally (first one group, or individual, and then another). When planning this, select phrases that lend heavier or darker feelings to be spoken by the deeper voices, or the group as a whole, and lighter phrases for individuals with higher voices. Songs may also be used as choral readings. Remember that, like music, this is a tool and not a performance.

Psalm 100 (GNB)

Leader: Sing to the Lord, all the world!
Group 1: Worship the Lord with joy;
Group 2: Come before him with happy songs!
Group 1: Acknowledge that the Lord is God.
Group 2: He made us, and we belong to him;
All: We are his people, we are his flock.
Group 1: Enter the Temple gates with thanksgiving; Go into its courts with praise.
Group 2: Give thanks to him and praise him.
Group 1: The Lord is good;
Group 2: His love is eternal
All: And his faithfulness lasts forever.

Using Storytelling to Tell the Story

Someone has said that the Bible is not a science book but rather a book telling us why God made the earth and how we are loved by God. The Hebrews knew the art of story-telling. For hundreds of years, they used storytelling to teach younger generations these aspects of God. Consequently, as Scripture was recorded it contained only the basic bones of the story.

Early writing materials also limited the amount of writing produced. In Bible times, it cost more than a day's wage to buy a single sheet of papyrus. As a nomadic people, they could not carry a large library of scrolls, and scrolls did not contain nearly the amount of material our modern, compact books do. The scripture writers gave the basic backbone of a story and left it to the storyteller to flesh it out.

Jesus must have been an excellent storyteller. Otherwise, people would not have left their work to spend hours listening to him. I can imagine him entertaining the crowd with the story of the Great Supper (Matthew 22:1-10), telling them in a stern voice, "The king was angry! And he sent his troops and destroyed those murderers and burned their city."

Turn to Luke 12:13-21 and read the story of the Rich Fool twice. The first time, read verse 20 as if God were passing judgment. The second time, read it with compassion and weeping. As you see, without the tone of the storyteller's voice, we do not get the full meaning of the story. Storytelling can make the difference in the way a story is received.

All stories contain *plot*, *place*, and *persons*. Like the legs of a milking stool, all three parts are needed to make the story complete. Mistakenly, we often think that the plot is the most important part, but often a plot is devised only to tell about the place or the person. Without the descriptive words, a story falls flat.

Suggestions for Learning a Story

1. Identify the four parts of the story (introduction, plot, climax, ending).
2. Get to know the characters, the customs of the time, and the location of the story.
3. Think about how the listener will relate to the characters and situations in the story.
4. Divide the story into blocks. Concentrate on each block and look at the connecting words between the blocks. Concentrate on the beginning and end of each block and on the whole story.
5. Repeat the story several times, "thinking" it as you do. You will want to internalize the story—to help it "leave" the page and become a part of you. Some people find it helpful to use a tape recorder as they practice. A storytelling partner is also helpful.

Suggestions for Telling the Story

1. A well-told story is better than a well-read story, but a well-read story is better than a poorly told story. The key is to know the story so well that it becomes a part of you, whether you are telling or reading it. If the only reason you are using the book is to follow the sequence, then write the sequence on a large sheet of paper and post it high on the wall above the listeners' heads. You will remember the sequence more easily if you have practiced it in blocks.

2. Consider any props and gestures that you will use. These will enhance the story. But any story should always be told as if the listener could not see the props and gestures. Be sure gestures are appropriate. In the story of Jesus healing the paralytic, Jesus asked the scribes, "Why do you question thus in your hearts?" If an accusing, pointing gesture is used, one message will be conveyed. However, if a gesture of opening the hands in puzzlement is used, then we see Jesus' question in another light, as concern over the scribes' attitude (Mark 2:1-12). Which attitude is more in keeping with Jesus' life and teachings?

3. Think about your tone of voice, facial expressions, and body posture. Happiness is heard in your tone as well as in your words.

4. Don't be afraid of pauses. Pauses give us time to think. They allow space in our thoughts for setting the stage.

5. Relax and enjoy the story. You will find that storytelling can bring you as much joy as it brings the listener.

(Adapted from Delia Halverson, *How to Train Volunteer Teachers* [Nashville: Abingdon Press, 1991], Handout 12.)

Storytelling is the most common way to help students "meet with" the story. Develop a variety of methods of storytelling. Include the student as often as possible.

Balloon Toss

Storytelling can involve the student as well as the teacher. For a balloon toss, write sections of the story on strips of paper. Insert each piece into a balloon. Stand in a circle and toss the balloons back and forth across the circle until a given signal. At the signal, each person takes a balloon and pops it. Then students read their section of the story to themselves and move into a line in the order of the story. When everyone has found his or her place, the story is read aloud in the sections.

NOTE: This same procedure can be done without the balloons. Simply mix up the story strips and pass them out.

Echo Pantomime

This is a simple way to tell the story and involve the students. See page 36 in chapter 6 for information on Echo Pantomime.

Flannel Board

When flannel boards were used forty or fifty years ago, they were strictly a spectator activity. Teachers today not only tell the story with flannel board figures, but they involve the students in the telling. Time is usually taken for students to tell and retell the story using the figures. Here is where the real learning takes place.

A flannel board can be simply made by covering a board or large piece of cardboard with a solid color of flannel or felt (usually black). Small pieces of flannel or felt are then glued to the backs of paper figures. The figures will stick to the board and can easily be moved about. Christian bookstores may also carry kits of flannel board characters.

From time to time, your curriculum will have a set of flannel board figures with the backs treated so that they stick to the board.

Recycle your curriculum and file these for future use. Pooling your flannel board stories with other teachers will give you a larger resource file.

Imagining

Consider interrupting your storytelling with an "Imagining Time." Tell the story up to a certain point. Then ask the students to imagine what they would do or say if they were the character at that point.

For example, the story of Zacchaeus could be told to the point where Zacchaeus comes down from the tree and meets Jesus. If you were Zacchaeus:

- What would you say?
- How could you make friends with Jesus?
- What would you tell Jesus about yourself so that he would know you better and you would be better able to be friends?

At this point you might suggest that the students draw a picture of themselves becoming friends with Jesus. After the pictures are completed, ask them to tell about the pictures. Now finish the Bible story (Luke 19:1-10).

Story Blocks and Story Chains

Story blocks and story chains can be great visual aids in storytelling. These have pictures to remind us of the parts in the story. For more information on these, turn to page 31 in chapter 5.

Litany

The story might be told as a litany. In a litany the leader, or individuals, read leading statements, and the whole group responds. Young children can use litanies if the response is always the same, or if it repeats the last few words of the sentence that the leader ends with. You can simplify this by putting a vocal emphasis on the words at the end of the sentence that you want repeated. Students who can read can use litanies that are written with different responses. Example:

The Big Flood
(Genesis 6:14, 19-22, 7:17, 8:1-20, 9:13-15)

Leader: God told Noah there would be a *big flood.*
Group: Big flood.
Leader: Noah was to build a *big ark.*
Group: Big ark.
Leader: The ark was a *big boat.*
Group: Big boat.
Leader: Noah brought animals *two by two.*
Group: Two by two.
Leader: Soon it rained and *rained hard.*
Group: Rained hard.
Leader: The waters rose and the *ark floated.*
Group: Ark floated.
Leader: It continued to rain for *forty days.*
Group: Forty days.
Leader: Noah sent a dove, and the *dove returned.*
Group: Dove returned.
Leader: He sent the dove again, and it returned *with a branch.*
Group: With a branch.
Leader: Soon the earth dried, and they *all came out.*
Group: All came out.
Leader: God made a promise and set a *rainbow in the sky.*
Group: Rainbow in the sky.
Leader: Noah built a special place and *thanked God.*
Group: Thanked God.

Pocket Chart

I have used the pocket chart often as a memorization aid for the Lord's Prayer or Bible verses. It can also be used to help students learn a simply told story. The pocket chart is made by taking poster board and creating long pockets along the board with folded strips of long paper, as explained below.

Supplies:
1 piece of poster board or heavy cardboard (22″ × 28″)
2 three-inch strips of paper (such as freezer or shelf paper), each 30 inches long
Transparent tape
Index cards (same number as there are words or phrases)

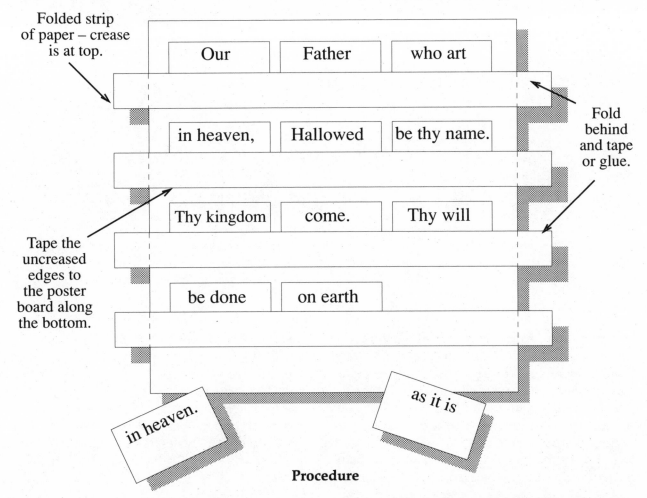

Folded strip of paper – crease is at top.

Fold behind and tape or glue.

Tape the uncreased edges to the poster board along the bottom.

Our   Father   who art

in heaven,   Hallowed   be thy name.

Thy kingdom   come.   Thy will

be done   on earth

in heaven.   as it is

Procedure

Fold the long strips of paper in half lengthwise. Placing the strips horizontally on the board with the crease facing down, space them evenly down the poster board taping the strips across the bottom and folding the ends around the edges of the poster board, taping them to secure (see illustration above).

Write words or phrases at the top of 3 × 5 cards, and place them in order in the pockets. Read the story as a class several times, using all the cards. Then each time you read the story, randomly remove one of the cards. Soon the class will be telling the story without the cards. (From Delia Halverson, *Teaching Prayer in the Classroom* [Nashville: Abingdon Press, 1989], pp. 24-25.)

If the group is small, you can create the same learning experience by simply placing the cards, face up, on the floor or table and removing cards as you learn the story.

Story Hat

One of my favorite ways of telling stories is to use a story hat. A story hat has miniature items attached to it that remind us of particular stories. Some teachers will use a story hat to recall familiar stories, adding the miniature item each time they tell a new story. The students may then look at the hat and choose what story they want retold. Or students can wear the hat themselves and tell the story.

I will also fix up a story hat at the beginning of a unit, with a different item on it representing each story to be used in the unit. The students must wait until the story is told to know what the miniature represents. This helps to create excitement over upcoming stories in a unit. I did this for a Vacation Bible School unit on Paul. The first story included his conversion and escape over the wall in a basket, and I used a small basket. The second story was about his first journey, which

included his stoning at Lystra, and so I used a small stone. The next day we studied his next two missionary journeys, so I made a small pair of cardboard sandals for the symbol. The last two stories were of his shipwreck and his letters. A paper boat and paper scrolls were appropriate for those stories (Acts 13–28).

Here are symbols for several other Bible stories:

Noah	Dove or rainbow
Baby Moses	Baby
Plagues	Frog
Jonah	Fish
Daniel	Lion
Nativity	Crèche
Jesus Feeding Multitude	Loaf of bread
Parable of Sower	Seed package
Lost Sheep (or 23rd Psalm)	Sheep

Story Tree

Jesse trees are popular items for reminding students of the stories of Jesus' heritage. Like the Jesse tree, the story tree uses the bare branch base, either placed in a flower pot with soil to support it, or mounted on the wall. Scrolls are made, each containing a Bible story. These are rolled up and tied to a small branch of the "tree." Each week a student selects a scroll story and reads it to the class.

Story Web

To spin a story web, divide the story into different sections, assigning these to different students. It is best if each person in the group has an assigned section. If the group is too large for this, ask those with assigned sections to space themselves around the circle. You may be sitting on the floor or in chairs, or standing in the circle. With young children it is best that you sit on the floor.

A ball of yarn is held by the student who was assigned the beginning of the story. He or she tells that part of the story, and then holds on to the end of the yarn or wraps it around the wrist and rolls or throws the ball to the person who has the next part of the story. That person tells that part and holds on to the yarn or wraps it around the wrist, throwing the ball across the circle to the next, and so on until the story is told. If there are persons who did not have a part in telling the story, ask them to reach out and take hold of the part of the web nearest them. Close the story by saying something like this: "We are all a part of God's story web. And all the people said 'Amen.' " Encourage the whole group to join you with this statement at the close of each use of the story web. Students may wish to take a part of the web yarn home to remind them of the story.

Treasure Hunt

In a treasure hunt, each person or group is given a clue to begin. That clue leads to a place where another clue has been hidden, and so forth until you reach the end, where the hidden treasure is found. For a storytelling version of this, divide the story into sections and write the story parts on cards. On the back of each card write the clue for locating the next part of the story. Before going on to the next clue, the student must read that part of the story. At the "treasure" location, place a small gift for each student. It might be something that is symbolic of the story.

Other Ways to Tell the Story

It has been said that our actions can cause new thinking much more easily than our thinking can cause new actions. Therefore, it is important that we teach experientially. In order to determine whether activities are experiential, consider whether the activity brings out how we feel about a situation more than what we think about it.

Atmosphere

You have already begun to tell the story when the first student walks into the room! When there are posters and pictures, or when a tent is set up in a section of the room, the atmosphere says, "Something exciting is happening here." You may simply use a blanket stretched across a rope for a tent, with cushions inside for seats. Refrigerator boxes can be cut apart and painted to look like the rock wall of a Palestinian home. Or a smaller appliance box can be used to make a rock well, with pottery jugs placed nearby. A flashlight shining through red cellophane paper placed under sticks makes the campfire a central focus as the student walks into the room.

Spend some time setting up your teaching area. Let your imagination work for you. Imagine just what it might have looked like at the time of the Bible story, and think of ways to re-create the atmosphere. If all is set and ready when the first student enters the room, then the student not only sparks with excitement, but he or she knows that the Bible is important to you and that you care enough to prepare ahead.

Archaeological Dig

Elementary children and youth will better understand the contributions of archaeologists if they can experience simulation. Using a large pan or box, place layers of sand in the bottom, burying small items between layers. These items will represent coins, lamps, water jars (or bits of pottery), statues, bracelets, mirrors, clay tablets, scrolls (or bits of paper). Have spoons and small brushes available, and allow students to remove sand, just a little at a time, to discover what is buried. Stress the fact that archaeologists must remove the dirt carefully so as not to spoil the treasures. Tell them that the location of the things they find is also important evidence in piecing together the past.

A youth class may want to do some research and spend time setting up such an archaeological dig for an elementary class to use.

Bookmarks

I use bookmarks in a classroom Bible with all ages. For the preschooler, I draw a picture on the bookmark that symbolizes a specific verse or story. I add the scripture reference to the bookmark for my own convenience. To make the bookmark, I either use a piece of paper or I draw the picture on half of a self-sticking label and then fold the label over, securing a ribbon between the two sides. The bookmark is then placed in the Bible and the scripture reference highlighted or underlined. A child can recognize the story or scripture passage by looking at the picture, and find it in the Bible and tell the story.

Elementary children and youth can make their own bookmarks. You might also have them make bookmarks like this for younger children to take home for use in their family Bibles.

Consider these symbols for simple scriptures:

Clouds or sunset	Psalm 19:1
Seashore	Psalm 95:5
Food	Job 36:31*b*
Grass	Psalm 104:14
Bethlehem with star	Luke 2
Loaves and fish	John 6:1-14
Sheep	Luke 15:3-7
Fish over open fire	John 21:1-13

Story Walk

A story walk tells the story in sections as you walk along a specific path. Make footprints out of colorful construction paper. On each "footstep" write a short section of the story in letters large enough to be read while standing. With masking tape, secure the footprints in step fashion, leading from the hallway into the room.

Or you may want to use washable chalk and write the story in sections of a sidewalk. As you walk along, you can read the story.

A dramatic way to devise a story walk is to set up scenes from the story (using persons in costume) around a large room, or in several rooms off a central hallway. Print posters for each scene that tell the part of the story the scene depicts. As persons approach each scene, they read the part of the story that goes with that scene. Some churches have used the same idea for a drive-through nativity scene, telling the story of the first Christmas. This is a special gift for the community.

Cooking and Eating

Cooking and eating are favorite things to do. The activity is certainly enjoyed intergenerationally! If you have a weekday preschool program and a group of older adults who meet at the church regularly on a weekday, consider planning a biblical meal together. One time have the children prepare the meal for the adults, and another time the adults can prepare it for the children.

Many youth groups regularly plan a special meal for older adults in the congregation. Suggest that they make one meal biblical, using foods that were typical of that time.

If you don't care to cook, you can simply use fresh fruits, particularly figs, cheeses, grape juice, and a flat bread or cracker.

There are several books with recipes for foods of Bible times. I keep a file of Bible time recipes. Many of them I have saved from old curriculum.

One fun recipe for students who are learning Bible skills is a Bible fruitcake (from *Prepare Our Hearts* by Muriel Tarr Kurtz. Copyright © 1986 by The Upper Room, 1908 Grand Avenue, P.O. Box 189, Nashville, TN 37202. Used by permission of the publisher).

Bible Fruitcake

1 cup Psalm 55:21 (use either or both)
2 cups Jeremiah 6:20 (last part of verse)
6 Job 39:14
3 tbsps. I Samuel 14:25
½ cup Judges 4:19 (first sentence)
4½ cups I Kings 4:22
2 tsps. Leviticus 2:13

2 tsps. Amos 4:5
½ tsp. II Chronicles 9:9
2 cups Numbers 17:8
2 cups both items in I Samuel 30:12, chopped to make 4 cups in all

Mix in large bowl in order given. The third item should be carefully and thoroughly beaten in. The last two items should be added by hand, possibly following Solomon's advice for making a good boy (Proverbs 23:14). If you follow that, you will have a good cake.

Bake at 250 degrees for two-and-a-half hours in four small oiled pans. You may line the pans with oiled, brown paper. Allow to cool in pans on sides or racks. Then, run a knife around the edges and turn out.

This is good eaten at once, but it gets better if wrapped in cheesecloth and soaked in fruit juice. Keep in a cool place.

(The ingredients are: butter or oil, sugar, eggs, honey, water, flour, salt, baking powder, spices—cloves, nutmeg, cinnamon—almonds, figs, and raisins.)

Passover (Seder) Meal

During Lent, particularly during Holy Week, you may want to enjoy a celebration of the Passover meal that Jesus had with his disciples in the upper room (Matthew 26:17-30). Remember that the Passover is a way of remembering when the Hebrews left Egypt (Exodus, selected), and how they followed Moses' instructions to sprinkle blood on their doors so that the angel of death would pass over their homes without harm. These are the special foods that they probably used:

Matzah This is an unleavened bread, or a bread made without yeast. Sometimes you can purchase this in a special foods section of the grocery store, or you may substitute crackers. Unleavened bread is used because the Hebrews left in such a hurry that they did not have time to let their bread rise.

Moror This means "bitter herbs" and reminds the Jews of how unhappy they were in Egypt. Horseradish is usually used here.

Karpers A green vegetable, usually parsley. This symbolizes new life, remembering that Passover is in the spring. The parsley is dipped in saltwater to remember the tears of the slaves.

Charoses To recall the mortar used by the slaves as they built the great cities for the Egyptians, a mixture of apples, nuts, and cinnamon is used. Sometimes raisins are also included. It is all chopped up fine and moistened with a little grape juice.

Pesach Lamb is the meat served, remembering that the night they left Egypt they killed a lamb and placed the blood on the door. We often substitute chicken.

If you would like to use the food in a ceremonial meal, include candles and juice. Here is a form you may want to follow:

Leader: We praise you, our God. You made the universe and all that is in it. We come to this feast of unleavened bread.
All: Glory be to you, O God. You give us light.

Light the candles on the table.

Leader: We celebrate the night that you, God, called us out of Egypt in such a hurry that we didn't even have time to let the bread rise. You came to us when we needed you.
All: Thank you, God, for showing your love.

The leader stands to offer a toast. All raise juice glasses to toast.

Leader: Blessed are you, our God, for the freedom you gave your people when they left Egypt.
All: And blessed are you, our God, for our freedom to worship you.

All drink juice. Leader holds up bread.

Leader: Bread is the staff of life. You give us bread, and you gave us life when you released us from Egypt.
All: We praise you, O God, for giving us life.
Youngest child: Why is this night different from all other nights?

Leader: Long ago, we were slaves of Pharaoh in Egypt. We were made to build cities with back-breaking labor. We cried out to God, and God set us free. Moses was our leader, and God caused Egypt's army to be covered by the sea after we passed through the sea onto dry ground.

All: We sing praises to you, God, for the victory.

Youngest child: What is the meaning of the lamb we eat?

Leader: Before our ancestors left, they followed God's direction and marked their doors with the blood of the lamb. Every firstborn of the families of Egypt died that night, but our houses were passed over and not one of our children died. We eat the paschal lamb, or pesach, to remember this.

Youngest child: What is the meaning of the unleavened bread?

Leader: When we left we did not have time to wait for the bread to rise, and so it was baked flat. This is the bread, or matzah, that reminds us of our freedom from slavery.

Pass the bread around, each breaking off a piece and eating.

Youngest child: What is the meaning of the fruit mixture?

Leader: The fruit mixture, or charoses, reminds us of the mortar that our ancestors used to build the cities for the Egyptians.

Youngest child: What is the meaning of the bitter herbs and parsley?

Leader: The bitter herbs, or moror, remind us of the unhappy lives we had as slaves. The parsley in saltwater reminds us of the many tears that fell while we were in Egypt.

Pass the bitter herbs and parsley to taste.

Leader: Give thanks to the Lord, for God is good.

All: God's love goes on forever.

Leader: Give thanks to God, who does great wonders.

All: God's love goes on forever.

Leader: Give thanks to our God, who made heaven and earth.

All: God's love goes on forever.

Leader: Give thanks to God, who brought us out of Egypt.

All: God's love goes on forever.

Leader: Give thanks to God, who is with us today.

All: God's love goes on forever. Amen.

At this point, eat the rest of the meal together.

Leader: The Lord bless you and keep you.

All: The Lord make his face to shine upon you . . . and give you peace. Amen. (Numbers 6:24-26)

Suggested Resources

Achtemeier, Paul, ed. *Harper's Bible Dictionary*. New York: Harper & Row, 1985.

Andre, Evelyn, ed. *Psalms and Songs*. Nashville: Graded Press, 1985.

_____. *Rejoice and Sing Praise*. Nashville: Abingdon, 1977.

_____. *Sing and Be Joyful*. Nashville: Abingdon, 1979.

Birnbaum, Stanley. *The Bible Alive*. Minneapolis: Winston Press, 1983.

Furnish, Dorothy Jean. *Experiencing the Bible with Children*. Nashville: Abingdon Press, 1990.

Griggs, Donald L. *Praying and Teaching the Psalms*. Nashville: Abingdon Press, 1984.

_____. *Translating the Good News Through Teaching Activities*. Nashville: Abingdon, 1980.

_____. *20 New Ways of Teaching the Bible*. Nashville: Abingdon, 1977.

Griggs, Patricia. *Opening the Bible with Children*. Nashville: Abingdon Press, 1986.

_____. *Using Storytelling in Christian Education*. Nashville: Abingdon, 1981.

Halverson, Delia. *Helping Your Child Discover Faith*. Valley Forge, Pa.: Judson Press, 1982.

_____. *Helping Your Teen Develop Faith*. Valley Forge, Pa.: Judson Press, 1985.

_____. *How to Train Volunteer Teachers*. Nashville: Abingdon Press, 1991.

_____. *Teaching Prayer in the Classroom*. Nashville: Abingdon Press, 1989.

Lien, Boyd. *Journey to Jerusalem*. Nashville: Abingdon Press, 1988.

Murray, Dick. *Teaching the Bible to Adults and Youth*. Nashville: Abingdon Press, 1987.

_____. *Teaching the Bible to Elementary Children*. Nashville: Discipleship Resources, 1990.

Smith, Judy Gattis. *26 Ways to Use Drama in Teaching the Bible*. Nashville: Abingdon Press, 1988.

_____. *Tell Me Some Stories About Jesus*. Colorado Springs, Col.: Meriwether, 1981.

Ward, Elaine M. *Growing with the Bible*. Brea, Calif.: Educational Ministries, 1986.

Williams, Michael E., ed. *A Storyteller's Companion* (in several volumes). Nashville: Abingdon Press, 1991.

Wright, Chris. *User's Guide to the Bible*. Batavia, Ill.: Lion, 1984.

Media Resources

Along the Road with Jesus (musical drama for elementary). Nashville: Graded Press.

Bethlehem B.C. (kit for Bible life experiences). Nashville: Graded Press.

Jesus Loves Us All (sound filmstrip, story block, posters). Nashville: Graded Press.

Marketplace 29 A.D. (notebook plan for Bible life experiences). Nashville: Abingdon.

Workers with God: In Bible Times and Today (filmslips, ages 3 and up). Nashville: Graded Press.

For the Student

Bible Info-Cards. Nashville: Graded Press, 1986.

Bull, Norman J. *100 Bible Stories.* Nashville: Abingdon, 1982.

Doney, Meryl. *How the Bible Came to Us.* Batavia, Ill.: Lion, 1985.

Dotts, Maryann. *When Jesus Was Born.* Nashville: Abingdon, 1979.

Dowley, Tim. *Moses and the Great Escape.* Chicago: Moody Press, 1987.

Gillespie, Mike. *Fun Old Testament Bible Studies* (youth). Loveland, Col.: Group Books, 1989.

Goddard, Carrie Lou. *Jesus.* Nashville: Abingdon, 1978.

Gustafson, Jean Louise, and Christine L. Poziemski. *Step by Step Through the Bible* (9–14 year olds). San Francisco: Harper & Row, 1984.

Ingram, Kristen Johnson. *Bible Stories for the Church Year.* San Francisco: Harper & Row, 1987.

Jones, Mary Alice. *The Bible Story of the Creation.* Chicago: Rand McNally, 1967.

Kostich, Beverly E. *Stepping into the Bible.* Nashville: Abingdon Press, 1988.

Parry, Linda and Alan. *Little Bible Story Books* (8 small books for preschoolers). Minneapolis: Augsburg, 1990.

_____. *Bible Families* (4 small books for early elementary). Minneapolis: Augsburg, 1990.

Ryan, John. *Mabel and the Tower of Babel.* Batavia, Ill.: Lion, 1990.

Savitz, Harriet May, and K. Michael Syring. *The Pail of Nails.* Nashville: Abingdon Press, 1989.

Spier, Peter. *Noah's Ark.* Garden City, N.Y.: Doubleday & Co., 1977.

Steptoe, John. *Mufaro's Beautiful Daughters* (African tale that gives message of Matt. 25:31-46). New York: Lothrop, Lee & Shepard Books, 1987.

Williamson, Nancy. *How Bible People Lived.* Minneapolis: Augsburg, 1983.

Index to Bible Stories
in the Text